Hans Breitmann's Ballads.

By Charles G. Leland.

Complete Edition In One Volume.

PHILADELPHIA:
T. B. PETERSON & BROTHERS;
306 CHESTNUT STREET.

Hans Breitmann's Party.

With Other Ballads.

BY CHARLES G. LELAND.

AUTHOR OF "HANS BREITMANN IN CHURCH, WITH OTHER NEW BALLADS," "HANS BREITMANN ABOUT TOWN," ETC., ETC.

First Series of the Breitmann Ballads.

PHILADELPHIA:
T. B. PETERSON & BROTHERS,
306 CHESTNUT STREET.

Contents.

Ad Musam.

"Est mihi schoena etenim et praestanti corpore liebsta:
Haec sola est mea Musa meoque regierit in Herzo,
Huic me ergebo ipsum meeque illi abstatto geluebda,
Huic ehrensaulas aufrichto opfroque Geschenka,
Hic etiam absingo liedros et carmina scribo."

Rapsodia Andra, Leipzig, 17th century.

Hans Breitmann's Party.

HANS BREITMANN gife a barty,
  Dey had biano-blayin;
I felled in lofe mit a Merican frau,
  Her name vas Madilda Yane.
She hat haar as prown ash a pretzel,
  Her eyes vas himmel-plue,
Und ven dey looket indo mine,
  Dey shplit mine heart in two.

Hans Breitmann gife a barty,
  I vent dere you'll pe pound.
I valtzet mit Madilda Yane
  Und vent shpinnen round und round.
De pootiest Fraeulein in de House,
  She vayed 'pout dwo hoondred pound,
Und efery dime she gife a shoomp
  She make de vindows sound.

Hans Breitmann gife a barty,
  I dells you it cost him dear.
Dey rolled in more ash sefen kecks
  Of foost-rate Lager Beer.
Und venefer dey knocks de shpicket in
  De Deutschers gifes a cheer.
I dinks dat so vine a barty,
  Nefer coom to a het dis year.

Hans Breitmann gife a barty;
  Dere all vas Souse und Brouse,
Ven de sooper comed in, de gompany
  Did make demselfs to house;
Dey ate das Brot and Gensy broost,
  De Bratwurst and Braten fine,
Und vash der Abendessen down
  Mit four parrels of Neckarwein.

Hans Breitmann gife a barty
  We all cot troonk ash bigs.
I poot mine mout to a parrel of bier
  Und emptied it oop mit a schwigs.
Und denn I gissed Madilda Yane
  Und she shlog me on de kop,
Und de gompany fited mit daple-lecks
  Dill de coonshtable made oos shtop.

Hans Breitmann gife a barty—
  Where ish dat barty now!
Where ish de lofely golden cloud
  Dat float on de moundain's prow?
Where ish de himmelstrahlende Stern—
  De shtar of de shpirit's light?
All goned afay mit de Lager Beer—
  Afay in de ewigkeit!

Breitmann in Battle.

"Tunc tapfre ausfuhrere Streitum et Rittris dignum potuere erjagere lobum."

DER FADER UND DER SON.

I dinks I'll go a fitin—outspoke der Breitemann,
"It's eighdeen hoonderd fordy eight since I kits swordt in hand;
Dese fourdeen years mit Hecker all roostin I haf been,
Boot now I kicks der Teufel oop and goes for sailin in."

"If you go land out-ridin," said Caspar Pickletongue,
"Foost ding you knows you cooms across some repels prave and young,
Away down Sout' in Tixey, dey'll split you like a clam"—
"For dat," spoke out der Breitmann, "I doos not gare one tam!"

Who der Teufel pe's de repels und vhere dey kits deir sass,
If dey make a run on Breitmann he'll soon let out de gas;
I'll shplit dem like kartoffels: I'll slog em on de kop;
I'll set de plackguarts roonin so dey don't know vhere to shtop."

Und den outshpoke der Breitmann, mit his schlaeger py his side:
" Forvarts, my pully landsmen! it's dime to run und ride;
Will riden, will fighten—der Copitain I'll pe,
It's sporn und horn und saddle now—all in de Cavallrie!"

Und ash dey rode troo Winchester, so herrlich to pe seen,
Dere coomed some repel cavallrie a riden on de creen;
Mit a sassy repel Dootchman—an colonel in gommand:
Says he, " Vot Teufel makes you here in dis mein Faderland?

" You're dressed oop like a shentleman mit your plackguard Yankee crew,
You mudsills and meganics! Der Teufel put you troo!
Old Yank you ought to shtay at home und dake your liddle horn,
Mit some oldt voomans for a noorse"—der Breitmann laugh mit shkorn.

" Und should I trink mein lager-bier und roost mine self to home?
Ife got too many dings like you to mash beneat' my thoom:
In many a fray und fierce foray dis Deutschman will be feared
Pefore he stops dis vightin trade—'twas dere he greyed his peard."

"I pools dat peard out by de roots—I gifes him sooch
a dwist
[tionist !
Dill all de plood roons out, you tamned old Apoli-
Your creenpacks mit your swordt und watch right ofer
you moost shell,
[h–ll !"
Und den you goes to Libby straight—und after dat to

"Mein creenpacks und mein schlaeger, I kits 'em in
New York,
[talk ;"
To gife dem up to creenhorns, young man, is not de
De heroes shtopped deir sassin' here und grossed deir
sabres dwice,
Und de vay dese Deutschers vent to vork vos von pig
ding on ice.

Der younger fetch de older such a gottallmachty smack
Der Breitmann dinks he really hears his skool go shplit
und crack ;
Der repel choomps dwelfe paces back, und so he safe
his life :
Der Breitmann says : "I guess dem choomps you
learns dem of your vife."

"If I should learn of vomans I dinks it vere a shame,
Bei Gott I am a shentleman, aristograt, and game.
My fader vos anoder—I lose him fery young—
Ter teufel take your soul ! Coom on ! I'll split your
waggin' tongue !"

A Yankee drick der Breitmann dried—dat oldt gray-
pearded man— [he ran.
For ash the repel raised his swordt, beneat' dat swordt
All roundt der shlim yoong repel's waist his arms oldt
Breitmann pound,
Und shlinged him down oopon his pack und laidt him
on der ground.

" Who rubs against olt kittle-pots may keep vite—if he
can, [man ?
Say vot you dinks of vightin now mit dis old shentle-
Your dime is oop; you got to die, und I your breest
vill pe ;
Peliev'st dou in Morál Ideas ? If so I lets you free."

" I don't know nix apout Ideas—no more dan pout
Saint Paul,
Since I peen down in Tixey I kits no books at all ;
I'm greener ash de clofer-grass ; I'm shtupid as a
shpoon ;
I'm ignoranter ash de nigs—for dey takes de *Tribune*.

" Mein fader's name vas Breitmann, I heard mein mut-
ter say,
She read de bapers dat he died after she rooned afay ;
Dey say he leaf some broperty—berhaps 'twas all a
sell—
If I could lay mein hands on it I likes it mighty well."

"Und vas dy fader Breitmann? *Bist du* his kit und kin?
Denn know dat *ich* der Breitmann dein lieber Vater bin?"
Der Breitmann poolled his hand-shoe off und shooked
him py de hand;
"Ve'll hafe some trinks on strengt of dis—or else may
I pe tam'd!"

"Oh! fader, how I shlog your kop," der younger
Breitmann said;
"I'd den dimes sooner had it coom right down on mine
own headt!"
"Oh, never mind—dat soon dry oop—I shticks him mit
a blaster; [der."
If I had shplit you like a fish, dat vere an vorse tisas-

Dis fight did last all afternoon—*wohl* to de fesper tide,
Und droo de streeds of Vinchesder, der Breitmann he
did ride. [tory!
Vot vears der Breitmann on his hat? De ploom of fic-
Who's dat a ridin' py his side? "Dis here's mein son,"
says he.

How stately rode der Breitmann oop!—how lordly he
kit down? [prown!
How glorious from de great *pokal* he drink de bier so
But der Yunger bick der parrel oop und schwig him
all at one. [mein son!"
"Bei Gott! dat settles all dis dings—I *know* dou art

Der one has got a fader ; de oder found a child.
Bote ride oopon one war-path now in pattle fierce und wild.
It makes so glad our hearts to hear dat dey did so succeed—
Und damit hat sein' Ende DES JUNGEN BREITMANN'S LIED.

Breitmann in Maryland.

DER Breitmann mit his gompany,
Rode out in Marylandt.
"Dere's nichts to trink in dis countrie;
Mine troat's as dry as sand.
It's light canteen und haversack,
It's hoonger mixed mit doorst;
Und if we had some lager-bier
I'd trink oontil I boorst.
Gling, glang, gloria!
We'd trink oontil we boorst.

"Herr Leut'nant, take a dozen men,
Und ride dis land around!
Herr Feldwebel, go foragin'
Dill somedings goot is found.
Gotts-doonder! men, go ploonder!
We hafn't trinked a bit
Dis fourdeen hours! If I had bier
I'd sauf oontil I shplit!
Gling, glang, gloria!
We'd sauf oontil we shplit!"

At mitternacht a horse's hoofs
Coom rattlin' troo de camp;
"Rouse dere!—coom rouse der house dere!
Herr Copitain—we moost tromp!
De scouds have found a repel town,
Mit repel davern near,
A repel keller in de cround,
Mit repel lager bier!!
Gling, glang, gloria!
All fool of lager-bier!

Gottsdonnerkreuzschockschwerenoth!
How Breitmann broked de bush!
"O let me see dat lager bier!
O let me at him rush!
Und is mein sabre sharp und true,
Und is mein war-horse goot?

To get one quart of lager bier
I'd shpill a sea of ploot.
Gling, glang, gloria!
I'd shpill a sea of ploot.

"Fuenf hoonderd repels hold de down,
One hoonderd strong are we;
Who gares a tam for all de odds
Wenn men so dirsty pe."
And in dey smashed and down dey crashed,
Like donder-polts dey fly,
Rush fort as der wild yæger cooms
Mit blitzen troo de shky.
Gling, glang, gloria!
Like blitzen troo de shky.

How flewed to rite, how flewd to left
De moundains, drees unt hedge;
How left und rite de yæger corps
Went donderin troo de pridge.
Und splash und splosh dey ford de shtream
Where not some pridges pe:
All dripplin in de moondlight peam
Stracks went de cavallrie!
Gling, glang, gloria!
Der Breitmann's cavallrie.

Und hoory, hoory on dey rote,
  Oonheedin vet or try;
Und horse und rider shnort und blowed,
  Und shparklin bepples fly.
Ropp! ropp! I shmell de barley-prew!
  Dere's somedings goot ish near.
Ropp! Ropp!—I scent de kneiperei;
  We've got to lager bier!
    Gling, glang gloria!
  We've got to lager bier!

Hei! how de carpine pullets klinged
  Oopon de helmets hart!
Oh, Breitmann—how dy sabre ringed;
  Du alter Knasterbart!
De contrapands dey sing for choy
  To see de rebs go down,
Und hear der Breitmann grimly gry:
  Hoorah!—we've dook de down.
    Gling, glang, gloria!
    Victoria, victoria!
  De Dootch have dook de down.

Mid shout and crash and sabre flash,
  And wild husaren shout
De Dootchmen boorst de keller in,
  Unt rolled de lager out;

And in the coorlin powder shmoke,
 While shtill de pullets sung.
Dere shtood der Breitmann, axe in hand,
 A knockin out de boong.
  Gling, glang, gloria!
  Victoria! Encoria!
 De shpicket beats de boong.

Gotts! vot a shpree der Breitmann had
 While yet his hand was red,
A trinkin lager from his poots
 Among de repel tead.
'Twas dus dey went at mitternight
 Along der moundain side;
'Twas dus dey help make history!
 Dis was der Breitmann's ride.
  Gling, glang, gloria;
  Victoria! Victoria!
  Cer'visia, encoria?
 De treadful mitnight ride
Of Breitmann's wild Freischarlinger,
 All famous, broad, und wide.

Breitmann as a Bummer.

DER Sheneral Sherman holts oop on his coorse.
He shtops at de gross-road und reins in his horse.
"Dere's a ford on de rifer dis day we moost dake,
Or elshe de grand army in bieces shall preak!"
Ven shoost ash dis vord from his lips had gone bast,
There coomed a young orterly gallopin fast,
Who gry mit amazement: "Here Shen'ral! Goot Lord!
Dat bummer der Breitmann ish holdin der ford!"

Der Shen'ral he ootered no hymn und no psalm,
But opened his lips und he priefly say "D——n!
Dere moost hafe been viskey on dat side der rifer;
To get it dose shaps would set hell in a shiver,
But now dat dey hold it, ride quick to deir aid:
Ho Sickles! move promp'ly, send down a prigade
Dat Dootchman moost work mighty hard mit his sword
If againsd a whole army he holds to de ford."

Dey spoored on, dey hoory'd on, gallopin shtraight,
But for Breitmann help coomed shust a liddle too late,
For ash de Lauwiné goes smash mit her pound,
So on to de Bummers de repels coom down:
Heinrich von Schinkenstein's tead in de road,
Dieterich Hinkelbein's flat ash a toad;
Und Sepperl—Tyroler—shpoke nefer a vord,
But shoost "*Mutter Gottes!"*—und died in de ford.

Itsch'l of Innspruck ish drilled troo de hair,
  Einer aus Bœblingen—he too vash dere—
Karli of Karlisruh's shot near de fence,
  (His horse vash o'erloadet mit toorkies und hens,)
Und dough he like a ravin mad cannibal fought,
  Yet der Breitmann–der capt'n–der hero vash caught;
Und de last dings ve saw, he was tied mit a cord,
  For de repels had goppled him oop at de ford.

Dey shtripped off his goat und skyugled his poots,
  Dey dressed him mit rags of a repel recruits;
But von grey-haared oldt veller shmiled crimly und bet
  Dat Breitman vouldt pe a pad egg for dem, yet.
"He has more on his pipe as dem vellers allows;
  He has cardts yet in hand und *das Spiel ist nicht aus*,
Dey'll find dat dey took in der teufel to board,
  De day dey pooled Breitmann well ofer de ford."

In de Bowery each bier-haus mit crape vas oop-done,
  Ven dey read in de bapers dat Breitmann vas gone;
Und de Dootch all cot troonk oopon lager und wein,
  At the great Trauer-fest of de Toorner Verein
Dere vas wein-en mit weinen ven beoples did dink
  Dat Sherman's great Sherman cood nefer more trink.
Und in Villiam Shtreet veepin und vailen vas hoor'd,
  Pecause der Hans Breitmann vas lost at de ford.

SECONDT PARDT.

IN *dulce jubilo* now ve all sings,
A-waivin de panners like avery dings.
De preeze troo de bine-drees ish cooler und salt,
Und der Shen'ral is merry venefer ve halt;
Loosty und merry he schmells at de preeze,
Lustig und heiter he looks troo de drees,
Lustig und heiter ash vell he may pe,
For Sherman, at last, has marched down to the sea!

Dere's a gry from de guart--dere's a clotter und dramp,
Ven dat fery same orterly rides troo de camp,
Who report on de ford. Dere ish droples and awe
In de face of de youf' apout somedings he saw;
Und he shpeak me in Fræntsch, like he always do:
"Look! [his spook!
Sagre pleu! fentre Tieu!—dere ish Breitmann—
He ish goming dis way! *Nom de garce!* can it pe
Dat de spooks of te tead men coom down to de sea!"

Und ve looks, und ve sees, und ve tremples mit tread,
For risin' all swart on de efenin red
Vas Johannes—der Breitmann—der war es, bei Gott!
Coom ridin to oos-ward, right shtrait to de shpot!
All mouse-still ve shtood, yet mit oop-shoompin hearts,
For he look shoost so pig ash de shiant of de Hartz;
Und I heard de Sout Deutschers say "Ave Morie!
Braise Gott all goot shpirids py land und py sea!"

Boot Itzig of Frankfort he lift oop his nose,
Und be-mark dat de shpook hat peen changin his clothes,
For he seemed like an Generalissimus drest
In a vlamin new coat and magnificent vest.
Six bistols beschlagen mit silber he wore,
Und a gold mounted swordt like an Kaisar he bore,
Und ve dinks dat de ghosdt—or votever he pe—
Moost hafe proken some panks on his vay to de sea.

"Id is he!" "*Und er lebt noch!* he lifes," ve all say:
Der Breitmann—Oldt Breitmann!—Hans Breitmann! *Herr Je!*"
Und ve roosh to emprace him, and shtill more ve find
Dat vherefer he'd peen, he'd left noding pehind.
In bote of his poots dere vas porte-moneys crammed,
Mit creen-packs stoof full all his haversack jammed,
In his bockets cold dollars were shinglin' deir doons
Mit two doozen votches und four doozen shpoons,
Und dwo silber tea-pods for makin' his dea,
Der ghosdt hafe pring mit him, *en route* to de sea.

Mit goot sweed-botatoes, und doorkies, und rice,
Ve makes him a sooper of avery dings nice.
Und de bummers hoont roundt apout, *alle wie ein*,
Dill dey findt a plantaschion mit parrels of wein.

Den t'vas "here's to you, Breitmann! Alt Schwed'—
bist zuruck?
Vot teufels you makes since dis fourteen nights week?"
Und ve holds von shtupendous und derriple shpree
For choy dat der Breitmann has got to de sea.

But in fain tid ve ashk vhere der Breitmann hat peen,
Vot he tid; vot he pass troo—or vot he might seen?
Vhere he kits his vine horse, or who gafe him dem woons,
Und how Brovidence plessed him mit tea-pods und shpoons?
For to all of dem queeries he only reblies
"If you dells me no quesdions, I ashks you no lies!"
So 'twas glear dat some derriple mysh'dry moost pe
Vhere he kits all dat ploonder he prings to de sea.

Dere ish bapers in Richmond dells derriple lies
How Sherman's grand armee hafe raise deir sooplies:
For ve readt *in brindt* dat der Sheneral Grant
Say de bummers hafe only shoost dake vat dey vant.
But 'tis vhispered dat vhile a refolfer'll go round
Der BREITMANN vill nefer a peggin' be found;
Or shtarvin' ash brisner—by doonder!—not he,
Vhile der teufel could help him to ged to de sea.

Breitmann in Kansas.

VONCE oopon a dimes, goot vhile afder der war vas ofer, der Herr Breitmann vent oud West, drafellin apout like afery dings—"*circuivit terram et perambulavit eam*," ash der Tyfel said ven dey ask him: "how vash you and how you has peen?"

Von efenings he vas drafel mit some ladies und shendlemans, und he shtaid *incognitus*. Und dey singed songs, dill py und py one of de ladies say: "Ish any podies here ash know de crate pallad of Hans Breitmann's Barty?" Den Hans say: "*Ecce Gallus!* I am dat rooster!" Den der Hans dook a trink und a let-bencil und a biece of baper, and goes indo himself a little dimes und denn coomes out again mit dis boem:

Hans Breitmann vent to Kansas;
  He drafel fast und far.
He rided shoost drei dousand miles
  All in von rail-roat car.
He knowed foost rate how far he goed—
  He gounted all de vile.
Dere vash shoost one bottle of champagne,
  Dat bopped at efery mile.

Hans Breitmann vent to Kansas;
  I dell you vot my poy.
You bet dey hat a pully dimes
  In crossin Illinoy.

Dey speaked dere speaks to all de folk
  A shtandin in de car;
Den ask dem in to dake a trink,
  Und corned em *ganz und gar.*

Hans Breitmann vent to Kansas;
  By shings! dey did it prown.
Ven he cot into Leafenvort,
  He found himself in town.
Dey dined him at de Blanter's House,
  More goot as man could dink;
Mit avery dings on eart to eat,
  Und dwice as mooch to trink.

Hans Breitmann vent to Kansas;
  He vent it on de loud.
At Ellsvort, in de prairie land,
  He foundt a pully crowd.
He looked for bleedin' Kansas,
  But dat's "blayed out," dey say;
De whisky keg's de only dings
  Dat's bleedin' der to-day.

Hans Breitmann vent to Kansas,
  To see vot he could hear.
He foundt soom Deutschers dat exisdt
  Py makin' lager bier.

Says he: "*Wie gehts du Alt Gesell?*"
  But no dings could be heard;
Dey'd growed so fat in Kansas
  Dat dey couldn't speak a vord.

Hans Breitmann vent to Kansas;
  Py shings! I dell you vot.
Von day he met a crisly bear
  Dat rooshed him down, *bei Gott!*
Boot der Breitmann took und bind der bear,
  Und bleased him fery much—
For efery vordt der crisly growled
  Vas goot Bavarian Dutch!

Hans Breitmann vent to Kansas!
  By donder dat is so!
He ridet out upon de plains
  To shase de boofalo.
He fired his rifle at the bools,
  Und gallop troo de shmoke,
Und shoomp de canyons shoost as if
  Der tyfel vas a choke!

It's hey de trail to Santa Fe;
  It's ho! agross de plain.
It's lope along de Denver road,
  Until we toorn again.

Und de railroad dravel after us
  Apout as quick as we;
Dis Kansas ish de fastest land
  Ash efer I did see.

Hans Breitmann vent to Kansas;
  He have a pully dime;
Bu 'tvas in oldt Missouri
  Dat dey rooshed him up sublime.
Dey took him to der Bilot Nob,
  Und all der nobs around;
Dey spreed him und dey tea'd him
  Dill dey roon him to de ground.

Hans Breitmann vent to Kansas;
  Troo all dis earthly land,
A vorkin out life's mission here
  Soobyectifly und grand.
Some beoblesh runs de beautiful,
  Some works philosophie;
Der Breitmann solfe de infinide
  Ash von eternal shpree!

Die Schœne Wittwe.

(DE POOTY VIDDER.)

Vot de Yankee Chap sung.

"DAT pooty liddle vidder
Vot we dosh'nt vish to name,
Ish still leben on dat liddle shtreet,
A-doin' shuss de same.
De glerks aroundt de gorners
Somedimes goes round to zee
How die tarlin liddle vitchy ees,
Und ask 'er how she pe.
Dey lofes her ver' goot liquœr,
Dey lofes her liddle shtore;
Dey lofes her liddle paby,
But dey lofes die vidder more.
To dalk mit dat shveet vidder,
Ven she hands das lager round,
Vill make der shap dat does id
Pe happy, ve'll be pound.
Dat ish if ve can vell pelieve
De glerks vat drinks das peer,
Who goes in dere for noding elshe,
Put simply for to zee her."

How der Breitmann cut him out.

OH yes I know die wittwe,
Mit eyes so prite und proun!
She's de allerschœnste wittwe
Vot live in dis here town.
In her plack silk gown—mine grashious!—
All puttoned to de neck—
Und a pooty liddle collar,
Mitout a shpot or shpeck.
Ho! clear de drack you oder *fraus*—
You cant pegin to shine
Ven de lofely vidder cooms along—
Dis vidder ash ish mine!
Ho! clear de drack you Yankee chaps,
You Englishers und sooch.
You cant pegin to coot me out,
Mit out you dalks in Dootch.
Ich hab die schœne wittwe
Schon lange nit gesehn,
Ich sah sie gestern Abend
Wohl bei dem Counter stehn.
Die Wangen rein wie Milch und Blut,
Die Augen hell und klar.
Ich hab sie sechsmal auch gekusst—
Potztausend! das ist wahr.

Breitmann and the Turners.

HANS BREITMANN choined de Turners
Novemper in de fall,
Und dey gifed a boostin' bender
All in de Toorner Hall.
Dere coomed de whole Gesangverein
Mit der Liederlich Aepfel Chor,
Und dey blowed on de drooms und stroomed on de fifes
Till dey couldn't refife no more.

Hans Breitmann choined de Toorners,
Dey all set oop some shouts,
Dey took'd him into deir Toorner Hall,
Und poots him a course of shprouts,
Dey poots him on de barrell-hell pars
Und shtands him oop on his head,
Und dey poomps de beer mit an enchine hose
In his mout' dill he's 'pout half-tead!

Hans Breitmann choined de Toorners;—
Dey make shimnastig dricks
He stoot on de middle of de floor,
Und put oop a fifdy-six.
Und den he trows it to de roof,
Und schwig off a treadful trink:
De veight coom toomple pack on his headt,
Und py shinks! he didn't vink!

Hans Breitmann choined de Toorners:—
  Mein Gott! how dey drinked und shwore
Dere vas Schwabians und Tyrolers,
  Und Bavarians by de score.
Some vellers coomed from de Rheinland,
  Und Frankfort-on-de-Main,
Boot dere vas only von Sharman dere,
  Und *he* vas a *Holstein* Dane.

Hans Breitmann choined de Toorners,
  Mit a Limpurg' cheese he coom;
Ven he open de box it schmell so loudt
  It knock de musik doomb.
Ven de Deutschers kit de flavor,
  It coorl de haar on dere head;
Boot dere vas dwo Amerigans dere;
  Und, py tam! it kilt dem dead!

Hans Breitmann choined de Toorners;
  De ladies coomed in to see;
Dey poot dem in de blace for de gals,
  All in der gal-lerie.
Dey ashk: "Vhere ish der Breitmann?"
  And dey drempla mit awe and fear
Ven dey see him schwingen py de toes,
  A trinken lager bier.

Hans Breitmann choined de Toorners:—
  I dells you vot py tam!
Dey sings de great Urbummellied:
  De holy Sharman psalm.
Und ven dey kits to de gorus
  You ought to hear dem dramp!
It scared der Teufel down below
  To hear de Dootchmen stamp.

Hans Breitmann choined de Toorners:—
  By Donner! it vas grand,
Vhen de whole of dem goes a valkin'
  Und dancin' on dere hand,
Mit de veet all wavin' in de air,
  Gottstausend! vot a dricks!
Dill der Breitmann fall und dey all go down
  Shoost like a row of bricks.

Hans Breitmann choined de Toorners,
  Dey lay dere in a heap,
And slept dill de early sonnen shine
  Come in at de window creep;
And de preeze it vake dem from deir dream,
  And dey go to kit deir feed:
Here hat' dis song an Ende—
  Das ist DES BREITMANNSLIED.

Ballad.

DER noble Ritter Hugo
Von Schwillensaufenstein,
Rode out mit shpeer and helmet,
Und he coom to de panks of de Rhine.

Und oop dere rose a meer maid,
Vot hadn't got nodings on,
Und she say, "Oh, Ritter Hugo,
Vhere you goes mit yourself alone?"

And he says, "I rides in de creenwood
Mit helmet und mit shpeer,
Till I cooms into em Gasthaus,
Und dere I trinks some beer."

Und den outshpoke de maiden
Vot hadn't got nodings on:
"I tont dink mooch ot beoplesh
Dat goes mit demselfs alone.

"You'd petter coom down in de wasser,
Vere deres heaps of dings to see,
Und hafe a shplendid tinner
Und drafel along mit me.

"Dere you sees de fisch a schwimmin,
Und you catches dem efery one:"—
So sang dis wasser maiden
Vot hadn't got nodings on.

"Dere ish drunks all full mit money
In ships dat vent down of old;
Und you helpsh yourself, by dunder!
To shimmerin crowns of gold.

"Shoost look at dese shpoons und vatches!
Shoost see dese diamant rings!
Coom down und full your bockets,
Und I'll giss you like avery dings.

"Vot you vantsh mit your schnapps und lager?
Coom down into der Rhine!
Der ish pottles der Kaiser Charlemagne
Vonce filled mit gold-red wine!"

Dat fetched him—he shtood all shpell pound;
She pooled his coat-tails down,
She drawed him oonder der wasser,
De maidens mit nodings on.

Hans Breitmann's Christmas.

"Hæc est illa bona dies
Et vocata læta quies
Vina sitientibus.

"Nullus metus, nec labores,
Nulla cura, nec dolores,
Sint in hoc symposio."

[*De Generibus Ebriosorum, Francoforti ad Mœnum, A. D.* 1565.]

ID vas on Weihnachtsabend—vot Ghristmas Efe dey call—
Der Breitmann mit his Breitmen tid rent de Musik Hall;
Ash de Breitmen und die vomen who were in de Liederkranz
Vouldt plend deir souls in harmonie to have a bleasin tantz.

Dey reefed de Hall 'mid pushes so nople to be seen,
Aroundt Beethoven's buster dey on-did a garlandt creen;
De laties vork like tyfels two days to scroob de vloor,
Und hanged a crate serenity mit Willkomm! oop de toor!

Und vhile dere vas a Schwein-blatt whose redakteur tid say:
Dat Breitmann he vas liederlich vet antworded dis-away,
Ve maked anoder serenity mid ledders plue und red:
"Our Leader lick de repels! N. G." (enof gesaid.)

Und anoder serene dransparency ve make de veller baint,
Boot de vay he potch und vertyfeled it vas enof to shvear a saint,

For ve vanted La Germania—boot der ardist mit a bloonder
Vent und vlorished Lager agross id—und denn poot Mania oonder !

Und as Ghristmas Efe was gekommen de beoples weren im Hall,
I shvears you id vas Gott-full—dat shplendit, pe-gloried ball?
Ve hat foon wie der Teufel in Frankreich—we coot oop like ter tyfel in France,
Und valk pair-wise in, while de musik blayed loudt de Fackel-Tanz.

But ven de valtz shtrike oopwart we most went out of fits,
Ash der Breitmann led off on a dwister mid de lofely Helmina Schmitz.
He valtz shoost like he vas shtandin shtill, mit a peaudiful solemn shmile,
Und 'Mina say he nafer shtop poussiren allaweil.

"Es tœnt, es rauschet Saitenklang—I hear de musik call
Den kerzenhellen Saal entlang—all troo de gleamin Hall,
O mœcht ich schweben stolz und froh—O mighdt I efer pe
Mit dir durchs ganze Leben so!—my Lebenlang by dee."

Und faster play de musik de Wellen und Wogen von
Strauss;
Und some drop into de tantzen und some of dem drop
aus;
Und soon like a shtorm in de Meere I feel de reelin vloor,
So de shpinners shtop mit de shpinsters, for dey couldn't
shpin no more.

Now weren ve all frolic, und lauter guter ding,
Und dirsty ash a broosh-pinder—ven ve hear some
glæsses ring;
Foorst mild und sonft in de distants—like de song of a
nightingoll,
Den a ringin und rottlin und clotterin—ash de Gluck
of Edenhall?

Hei! how we roosh on de liquor!—hei! how de kell-
ners coom!
Hei! how we busted de bier kegs und poonished de
Punsch a la Rhum,
Like lonely wafes at mitternight oopon some shiant
shore;
Like an awful shtorm in de Wælder—was de dirsty
Deutschers' roar!

I pyed some carts for a dime abiece—I pyed shoost
fifdy-dwo.
Dey were goot for bier, or schnapps, or wein—py don-
der how dey flew!

I ring de deck on de vaiters for liquor hot und cool,
Und avery dime I blays a cart, py shings, I rake de pool!

Und ash ve trinked so comforble, like boogs in any roog,
De trompets blowed *tan da ra dei,* und dere coom in a Maskenzug,
A peaudiful brocession, soul-raisin und sooplime,
De marmorbilds of de heroes of de early Sherman dime.

Dere vent der gross Arminius, mit his frau Thusnelda, too,
De vellers ash lam de Romans dill dey roon mit noses plue,
Den vollowed Quinctilius Varus, who carry a Roman yoke,
Und arm-in-arm mit Gambrinus come der Allemane Chroc.

Der alte Friedrich Rothbart, und Kaiser Karl der crate,
Mit Roland und Uliverus ven shveepin on in shtate;
Und Conradin whose sad-full deat' shtill makes our heartsen pleed,
Und all of dem oldt vellers aus dem Niblungen Lied.

Und as dey mofed on, der Breitmann maked a tyfeled shplendid witz
In anti-word to dis quesdion from de lofely 'Mina Schmitz:

"Vy ish id dey always makes in shtone dem vellers so andiquatet?"
"Vy—dey set in de laps of Ages dill dey got lapidated!"

Und shoost ash de last of dis hisdory hat fonished troo de toor,
Ve heardt a ge-screech, und Pelz Nickel coom howlin on de vloor;
Den de laties yell like der tyfel, und vly like gulls mit vings,
Und der Peltz Nickel lick em mit svitches und ve laughed like averydings.

I nefer hafe sooch laughen before dat I was geborn,
Und Pelz Nickel ven 'twas ober he blow on a yæger horn
Und denounce do all de beople gesembled in de hall:
Dat a Ghristmas dree vas vaiten mit bresents for oos all!

So ve vollowed him into de zimmer so quick ash dese vords he said,
To kit dem peaudiful bresents, all gratis und on de dead,
Und in facdt a shplendid Weihnachtsbaum mid lighds ve druly found,
Und liddel kifts dat ge-kostet a benny abiece all round!

Dere vas Rika Stange die Dessauerinn—a maedchen shtraigdt und tall,
She got a bicture of Cupid—boot she didn't see it at all

Dill der Breitmann say mit his shplendid shtyle dat all
de laties dake:
"Dat pend of de bow is de Crecian pend dat you so
ofden make!"

Anoder scharmante laty, Maria Top, did got
A schwingin mid a ribbon, a liddle benny pot;
Boot Breitmann hafe id de roughest of any oder mans,
For he kit a yellow gratle mit a liddle wooden Hans.

Den next Beethoven's Sinfonie, die orkester did blay;
Adagio—allegro—andante cantabile.
We sat in shtill commotion so dat a bin mighdt drops,
Und de deers roun town der Breitmann's sheeks mit-
whiles he was trinkin schnapps.

Next dings ve had de Weinnachtstraum gesung by de
Liederkranz.
Denn I trinked dwelf schoppens of glee wine to sed me
oop for a tanz;
Dis dimes I tanz wie der Tyfel—we shriek de volk on
de vloor;
Und boost right indo de sooper room—for ve tanzt a
hole troo de door!

Denn 'twas rowdy tow und hop-sossa, ve hollered, Mann
und Weib;
"Rip Sam und sed her oop acain!—ve're all of de
Shackdaw tribe!"

Venn Pelz Nickel blow his trump once more, und peg
peg oos to shtop our din,
Und troo de open toor dere comed nine denpins
marchin in.

Nine vellers tressed like denpins—dey goed to der end'
der hall,
Und dwo Hans Wurst, shack-puddin glowns—dey rolled
at em mit a pall.
De palls vas painted peaudiful; dey vas vifdeen feet
aroundt;
Und de rule of de came : whoefer cot hidt moost doom-
ple on de croundt.

Somedimes dey hit de denpins—somedimes de oder
volk—
Und pooty soon de gompany was all laid out in shoke;
Boot I tells you vot it makes oos laugh dill ve py nearly
shplits,
Ven der Breitmann he roll ofer and drip up de Mina
Schmitz.

Dis lets itself in Sherman pe foost-rade word-blayed on,
Und mongst oos be giftet vellers you pet dat it vas tone!
How der Breitmann mighdt drafel as brideman on de
roadt dat ish *breit* and *krumm;*
Here de drumpets soundt, and pair-wise ve goed for de
sooper room.

Ve goed for ge-roasted Welsh-hens, ve goed for ge-
spickter hare,
Ve goed for kartoffel salade mit butter brod—Kaviar;
Ve roosh at de lordtly sauer-kraut und de wurst vich
lofely shine,
Und oh mein Gott in Kimmel! how we goed for de
Mosel-wein!

Und troonker more, und troonker yet, und troonker shtill
got ve,
In rosy lighdt shtill drivin on agross a fairy see;
Den madder, wilder, frantic-er I proked a salat dish!
Und shoost like roarin elefants ve tanzt aroundt de tish.

I'fe shvimmed in heafenly troonks pefore—boot nefer
von like dis,
De morgen-het-ache only seemt a bortion of de bliss.
De while in trilling peauty roundt like heafenly vind-
harps rang
A goosh of golden melodie — de Rhineweinbechers
Klang.

De meltin minnesingers song—a droonk of honeyd
rhyme—
De b'wildrin-dipsy Bardic shants of Teutoburgic dime,
Back to de runic dim Valhall und Balder's foamin
mead;
——Here ents in heller glorie schein des Breitmann's
Weihnachtslied!

Der Freischuetz.

WIE geht's my frients—if you'll allow,
I sings you rite avay shoost now
Some dretful shdories vitch dey calls
DER FREYSCHUETZ; or, de Magic Balls.

Wohl in Bohemian land it cooms,
Where folks trinks prandy mate of plums;
Dere lifed ein Yager—Maxerl Schmit,
Who shot mit goons and nefer hit.

Und dere vas one old Yager, who
Says, " Maxerl, dis vill nefer do;
If you should miss on trial day,
Dere'l pe de tyfel den to pay.

" If you do miss, you shtupid goose,
Dere'l pe de donnerwetter loose;
For you shant have mine taughter's hand,
Nor pe de Hertshog's yagersmann."

It coomed pefore de day was set,
Dat all de chaps togeder met,
Und Maxerl fired his bix and missed,
Und all de gals cot round and hissed.

Dey laughed pefore, and hissed pehind;
Put one chap, Kaspar, set: "tont mind!
I dells you what, you stuns 'em alls,
If yoost you shoot mit magic palls."

"De magic palls—oh vot is dat!"
"I got dem in mine hoontin hat;
De're plack as kohl und shoot so true,
Oh dems de sort of palls for you.

"You see dat eagle flyin high,
Ein hoondred miles up in de sky?
Shoot at dat eagle mit your bix,
You kills him dead as doonderblix."

"I tont pelieve de dings you say."
"You fool," says Kass, "den plaze avay!"
He plazed avay, ven sure as blood,
Down coomed de eagle in de mud.

"*O was ist das?*" said Maxerl Schmit,
"Vy—dat's de eagle vat you hit.
You kills um vhen you plaze avay;
But dat's a ting you nix ferstay.

"Und you moost go to make dem balls
To de Wolf's Glen ven mitnight falls;
Dow knowst de shpot?—alone and late"—
"O ja—I knows him *ganz* foost-rate."

"But denn I does not likes to go
Among dem dings." Says Kass, "Ach sho!
I'll help you fix dem tyfel chaps;
Like a goot fellow—take some schnapps!

"(*Hilf Zamiel! hilf!*)—Here, trink some more!"
Den Kass vent shtomping roundt de floor,
Und coomed his hoomboogs ofer Schmit,
Till Max said "*Nun—ich gehe mit!*"

All in de finster mitternockt,
When oder folks in shleep vas locked,
Down in de *Wolfsschlucht* Kass did try
His tyfel-strikes und *hexerei*.

Mit skools and pones he made a ring,
De howls and spooks pegin to sing;
Und all de tyfels oonter ground
Coome breaking loose and rushin round.

Den Maxerl cooms along; says he,
"Mein Gott! what dings is dis I see!
I dinks de fery tyfel und all
Moost help to make dem magic pall.

"I vish dat I had nix cum rous,
Und shtaid mineself in bett to house."
"*Hilf Zamiel!*" cried Kass, "you whelp!
You red Dootch tyfel—coom und help!"

Den up dere coomed a tredful shtorm,
De todtengrips aroundt did schwarm;
De howl joomped oop und flapt his vings,
Und turned his het like averydings.

Up troo de groundt here coomed a pot,
Mit leadt und dings to make de shot;
Und hœllisch fire in crimson plaze,
Und awful schmells like Schweitzer kæs'.

Across de scene a pine shtick flew,
Mit seferal jail-pirds fastent to,
Six treadful jail-birds, mit deir vings
Tied to de shticks mit magic shtrings.

All troo de air, all in a row,
Die wilde Jagd was seen to go;
De hounts und deer all made of pone,
Und hoonted by a skilleton.

Dere coomed de dretful shpectre pig
Who shpitten fire, away did dig;
Und fiery drocks und tyfel-snake
A scootin troo de air tid preak.

But Kass he tidn't mind dem alls,
But casted out de pullet palls;
Six was to go as dey wouldt like,
De sevent moost for de tyfel strike.

At last oopon de trial day
De gals coomed round so nice and gay;
Und denn dey goes and makes a tanz
Und stinged apout de *Jungfernkranz.*

Und denn der Hertshog—dat's de Duke—
Cooms down und dinks he'll take a look;
"Young mans," to Maxerl denn says he,
"Shoost shoot dem dove upon dat dree!"

Denn Maxerl pointed mit de bix—
"Potzblitz!" says he, "dat dove I'll fix!"
He fired his rifle at de *Taub,*
When Kass rolled over in de *Staub.*

De pride she falled too in de dust,
De gals dey cried—de men dey cussed:
De Hertshog says, "It's fery clear
Dat dere has peen some tyfels here;

"Und Max has shot mit tyfels-*blei.*
Pfui!—die verfluchte Hexerei!
O Maximilian! O du
Gehst nit mit rechten Dingen zu!"

But den a hermits coomed in late,
Says he, "I'll fix dese dings foost-rate."
Und telld de Hertshog dat young men
Will raise der tyfel now and denn.

De Duke forgifed de Kaspar dann
Und made of him ein Yagersmann,
What shoots mit bixen gun and pfeil,
Und talks apout de *Waidmannsheil.*

Und denn de pride she coomed to life,
Und cot to pe de Maxerl's wife ;
Den all de beoples cried Hoorah !
Das ist recht brav ! und hopsasa !

MORAL.

Py dis dings may pe oondershtood
Dat vhat is pad vorks ofden goot :
Or, *Maximilia Maximil-*
ibus curantur—if you will.

Hans Breitmann About Town.

And Other New Ballads.

By Charles G. Leland.
Author of "Hans Breitmann's Party," etc.

Second Series of the Breitmann Ballads.

PHILADELPHIA:
T. B. PETERSON & BROTHERS;
306 CHESTNUT STREET.

RINGWALT & BROWN, PRS.

Contents.

Breitmann about Town.

DER Schwackenhammer coom to down,
  Pefore de Fall vas past,
Und by der Breitmann drawed he in
  Ash dreimals honored gast.
Led's see de sighdts! In self und worldt,—
  Dere's "sighdts" for him, to see,
Who Selbstanschaungsvermœgen hat,
  Said Breitemann, said he.

Dey vented to de Opera Haus,
  Und dere dey vound em blayin'.
Of Offenbach, (der *open brook,*)
  His show spiel Belle Heléne.
"Dere's Offenbach,—Sebastian Bach,—
  Mit Kaulbach,—dat makes dree:
I alvays likes soosh *brooks* ash dese."
  Said Breitemann, said he.

Dey vented to de Bibliothek,
  Vhich Mishder Astor bilt:
Some pooks vere only *en broschure*,
  Und some vere pound und gilt.
"Dat makes de gold—dat makes de *sinn*,
  Mit pooks, ash men, ve see,
De pest tressed vellers gilt de most:"—
  Said Breitemann, said he.

Dey vent to see an edider,
 Who'd shanged his flag und doon,
Und crowed oopon der oder side,
 Dat very afdernoon.
"De anciends vorshipped wetter-cocks,
 To wetter *fanes* pent de knee;
Pow down, mein Schwackenhammer, pow!"
 Said Breitemann, said he.

Dey vented py a panker's hause,
 Und Schwackenhammer shvore,
Id only vant a pig *red shield*
 Hoong oop pefore de toor;
One side of red, one side of gold,
 Like de knighd's in hisdorie—
"De schildern of dat schild is rich,"
 Said Breitemann, said he.

Dey vent oonto a bicture sale,
 Of frames wort' many a cent,
De broberty of a shendleman,
 Who oonto Europe vent.
"Dont gry—he'll soon pe pack again
 Mit anoder gallerie:
He sells dem oud dwelf dimes a year,"
 Said Breitemann, said he.

Dey vented to dis berson's house,
  To see his furnidure,
Sold oud at aucdion rite afay,
  Berembdory und sure.
"He geeps six houses all at vonce
  Each veek a sale dere pe,
Gotts! vat a dime his vife moost hafe!"—
  Said Breitemann, said he.

Dey vent to vind a goot cigar,
  Long dimes dey roamed apout,
Von veller had a pran new sort,
  De fery latest out.
"Mein freund—I dinks you errs yourself
  De shmell ish oldt to me;
De *Infamias Stinkadores* brand,"-
  Said Breitemann, said he.

Dey vented to de *virst* hotel,
  De prandy make dem creep,
A trop of id's enough to make
  A brazen monkey veep.
"Dey say a viner house ash dis,
  Vill soon ge-bildet pe,
Crate Gott!—vot *can* dey mean to trink?"
  Said Breitemann, said he.

Dey vented droo de Irish shtreeds,
  Dey saw vrom haus to haus,
Und gountet oop, 'pout more or less,
  Vive hoondred awful rows.
"If all dese liddle vights dey waste,
  Could *von* crate pattle pe,
Gotts! how de Fenian funds vouldt rise!"
  Said Breitemann, said he.

Dey vent to see de Ridualisds,
  Who vorship Gott mitt vlowers,
In hobes he'll lofe dem pack again,
  In winter among de showers.
"Vhen de Pacific railroat's done
  Dis dings imbrofed vill pe,
De joss-sticks vill pe santal vood,"—
  Said Breitemann, said he.

Dey vent to hear a breecher of
  De last sensadion shtyle,
'Twas 'nough to make der tyfel weep
  To see his "awful shmile."
"Vot bities dat der Fechter ne'er
  Vas in Theologie.
Dey'd make him pishop in dis shoorsh,"
  Said Breitemann, said he.

Dey vent indo a shpordin' crib,
  De rowdies cloostered dick,
Dey ashk him dell dem vot o'glock,
  Und dat infernal quick.
Der Breitmann draw'd his 'volver oud,
  Ash gool ash gool couldt pe,
"Id's shoost a goin' to shdrike six,"
  Said Breitemann, said he.

Dey vent polid'gal meedins next,
  Dey hear dem rant and rail,
Der bresident vas a forger,
  Shoost bardoned oud of jail.
He does it oud of cratitood,
  To dem who set him vree :
"Id's Harmonie of Inderesds,"
  Said Breitemann, said he.

Dey vent to a clairfoyand witch,
  A plack-eyed handsome maid,
She wahrsagt all der vortunes—denn
  "Fife dollars, gents!" she said.
"Dese vitches are nod of dis cart',
  Und yed are *on* id, I see
Der Shakesbeare knew de preed right vell,"
  Said Breitemann, said he.

Dey vented to a restaurand,
  Der vaiter coot a dash ;
He garfed a shicken in a vink,
  Und serfed id at a vlash.
"Dat shap knows vell shoost how to coot,
  Und roon mit poulterie,
He vas copitain oonder Turchin vonce,"
  Said Breitemann, said he.

Dey vented to de Voman's Righds,
  Vere laties all agrees,
De gals should pe de voters,
  Und deir beaux all de votées.
"For efery man dat nefer vorks,
  Von frau should vranchised pe :
Dat ish de vay I solf dis ding,"
  Said Breitemann, said he.

Dey vented oop, dey vented down,
  'Tvas like a roarin' rifer,
De sighds vas here—de sighds vas dere—
  Und de vorldt vent on forefer.
"De more ve trinks, de more ve sees,
  Dis vorldt a derwisch pe ;
Das Werden's all von whirling droonk,"
  Said Breitemann, said he.

Schnitzerl's Philosopede.

PARDT SECONDT.

VEN Breitmann hear dat Schnitzerl
  Vas quardered into dwo,
Und how his crate philosopede
  To 'm teufel had gone flew;
He dinked and dinked so heafy
  As only Deutschers can,
Denn saidt, "Who mighdt beliefet
  Dis ish de ent of man?

"De human souls of beoples
  Exisdt in deir ideés,
Und dis of Wolfram Schnitzerl
  Mighdt dravel many vays,
In his *Bestimmung des Menschen*
  Der Fichte makes peliefe
Dat ve brogress oon-endly
  In vot pehind we leafe.

"De shbarrow falls ground-downwarts.
  Or drafels to de West;
De shbarrows dat coom afder
  Bild shoost de same oldt nest.
Man hat not vings or fedders,
  Und in oder dings, 'tis saidt,

He tont coom oop to shbarrows;
   Boot on nests he goes ahet.

"O vliest dou troo bornin vorldts
   Und nebuloser foam,
By monsdrous mitnight shiant forms
   Or vhere red tyfels roam,
Or vhere de chosts of shky rackets
   Peyond creadion flee?
Vhere'er dou art, oh Schnitzerlein!
   Crate saint! look down on me!

"Und deach me how you maket
   Dat crate philosopede,
Vitch röon dwice six mals vaster
   Ash any Arap shteed,
Und deach me how to 'stonish folk
   Und knock dem out de shpots.
Come pack to eart, O Schnitzerlein,
   Und pring it down to dots!"

Shoost ash dis vort vent outvarts
   Hans dinked he see a vlash,
Und unterwards de dable
   He doomple mit a crash,
Und to him, moong de glaesses,
   Und pottles ash vas proke,
Mit his het in a cigar box,
   An foice from Himmel shpoke:

"*Adsum Domine* Breitmann!
Herr Capitain—here I pe!
So dell me right *honesté*
Quare inquietasti me?
Te video inter spoonibus,
Et largis glassis too,
Cerevisia repletis,
Sicut percussus tonitru!"

Denn Breitmann ansver Schnitzerl:
"*Coarctor nimis.*—See!
Siquidem Philistiim
Pugnant adversum me.
Ergo vocavi te,
Ash Saul *vocavit* Sam-
uel, *ut mi ostenderes*
Quid teufel *faciam?*"

Denn der shpirit, in Lateinisch
Saidt "*Bene*—dat's de dalk!
Non habes in hoc shanty
A shingle *et* some chalk?
Non video inkum et calamos:
(I shbose some bummer shdole 'em):
Levate oculos tuos, son
Et aspice ad linteolum!"

Den Breitmann see de chalk-piece
  Vitch riset from de floor,
Und signet a philosopede
  Alone oopon de toor,
De von dat Schnitzerl fabricate,
  Und oonderneat he see :
Probate inter equites :
  " Try dis in de cavallrie."

Den Breitmann shtoot ooprightly
  Und leanet on a bost,
Und saidt ; " If dis couldt, shouldt hafe [peen
  It vouldt mighdt peen a chost !
Boot if it pe nouomenon,
  Phenomenoned indeed,
Or de soobyective obyectified,
  I'fe cot de philosopede."

Denn out he seekt a plack schmidt
  Ash vork in iron shteel ;
To make him a philosopede
  Mit shoost an only vheel.
De dings vas maket simple,
  Ash all crate ideés should pe ;
For 'twas noding boot a gart vheel
  Mit a two veet achsel-dree.

De dimes der Breitmann doomple
  In learnin for to ride,
Vas ofdener ash de sand grains
  Dat rollen in de tide.
De dimes he cot oopsetted
  In shdeerin lefdt und righdt,
Vas ofdener as de cleamin shdars
  Dat shtud de shky py nighdt.

Boot de vorstest of de veadures
  In dis von vheel horse, you bet,
Ish dat man couldt go so nicely
  Pefore he got oopset,
Some dimes he go like plazes
  Und toorn her, extra-fein,
Und denn shlop ofer—dis is vhat
  Hafe kill der Schnitzerlein.

Soosh droples as der Breitmann hafe
  To make dis 'vention go,
Vas nefer seen py mordal man
  Oopon dis vorldt pelow.
He doompled righdt, he doompled lefdt,
  He hafe a tousand toomps,
Dere nefer vas a gricket-ball
  Vot got soosh 'fernal boomps.

Boot ash he shvear't he'd do it,
He shvore id should pe done,
Dough he schimpft und fluchte laesterlich,
He visht he'd ne'er pegun.
Mit *Hagel! Blitz! Kreuzsakrament!*
He maket de houser ring,
Und hoped de Schnitzerl pe verdammt
For deachin him dis ding.

Nun—goot! Ad last he got it.
Und peaudifool he goed,
Dis day, saidt he, " I'll stonish folk
A ridin on de road;
Dis day py shinks I'll do it!
Und knock dings out of sight!"
Ach weh! for Breitmann dat day
Vas not pe-markt mit vhite.

De noompers of de Deutsche folk
Dat coom dis feat to see,
I dink in soper earnest-hood,
Mighdt not ge-reckonet pe.
For miles dey shtood along de road,
Mein Gott! but dey vas dry;
Dey trinked den lager-beer shops oop,
Pefore der Hans coom py.

Vhen all at vonce drementous gries
  De fery country shook ;
Und beoples shkreemt : " *Da ist er ! Schau !*
  Dere ish der Breitmann !—Look !"
Mein Gott ! vas efer soosh a shoudt ?
  Vas efer soosh a gry ?
Ven like a brick-bat in a vight,
  Der Breitemann roosh py.

O mordal man ! Vy ish id, dow
  Hast passion to go vast ?
Vy ish id dat de tog und horse
  Likes shbeed too quick to last ?
De pugs, de pirds, de pumple-pees,
  Und all dat ish, 'twould seem,
Ish nefer hoppy boot, exsept
  When pilin on de shteam.

Der Breitmann flew ! Von mighdy gry,
  Ash he vent scootin bast,
Von derriple, drementous yell—
  Dat day de virst—and last.
Vot ha ! vot ho ! Vy ish id dus ?
  Vot makes dem shdare aghast ?
Vy cooms dat vail of wild tespair ?
  Ish somedings got gesmasht ?

Yea—efen so. Yea, ferily—
  Shbeak, soul! It is dy biz!
Der Breitmann shkeet so vast along,
  Dey fairly heard him whizz.
Ven shoost oopon a hill-top point
  It caught a pranch ge-pent,
Und like an opple vrom a svitch,
  Afay Hans Breitmann vent.

Vent troo de air a hoondert feet,
  (Allowin more or less)—
Denn *pobb—pobb—pobb*—a mile or dwo,
  He rollet along—I guess.
Say—hast dou seen a gannon ball
  Half shpent, shtill poundin on;
Like made of gummi-lasticum?
  So vent der Breitemann.

Dey bick him up—dey pring him in—
  No wort der Breitmann shpoke.
Der doktor look—he shvear erstaunt
  Dat nodings ish peen proke!
He rollet de rocky road entlong,
  He pouncet o'er shtock und shtone?
You'd dink he'd knocked his outsides in,
  Yet nefer preak a pone!

All shtill Hans lay—bevilderfied—
  Nor seemet to mind de shaps,
Nor moofed, oontil der medicus
  Hafe dose him vell mit schnapps.
De schmell voke oop de boetry
  Of tays ven he vas young,
Und he murmulte de frogmends
  Of an sad romandic song :

" As summer pring de roses,
  Und roses pring de dew,
So Deutschland gifes de maidens
  Vot fetch de bier to you.
Komm Maidlein ! Rothe Wænglein !
  Mit a wein glass in your paw !
Ve'll ged troonk amoong de roses
  Und lie soper on de shdraw !

" As winter prings de ice-wind,
  Dat plow o'er burg und hill,
Hard times pring in de lantlord,
  Und de lantlord pring de bill.
Boot sing Maidlein ! Rothe Wængelein !
  Mit wein glass in your paw !
Ve'll ged troonk amoong de roses
  Und lie sober on de shdraw !"

Dey dook der Breitmann homewarts,
  Boot efer on de vay,
He nefer shbeaket no man,
  Und noding else could say:
Boot—"Maidlein—Rothe Wængelein!
  Mit wein glass in her paw,
We'll ged troonk amoong de rosen
  Und lie soper on de shdraw!"

Dey laid der Hans im Bette,
  Peneat de eider-doun,
Und sempled all de doktors
  Vot doktored in de town.
Dat ish, de Deutsche Aertzte,
  For Breitmann alfays says,
De Deutschers ish de onlies
  Mit originell idées.

Dere vas Doktor Moritz Schlinkenschlog,
  Dat vork ash caféopath,
Und der learned Cobus Schoepfskopf,
  Dat use de milchy bath;
Und Korschalitschky aus Boehmen,
  Vot cure mit slibovitz,
Und Wechselbalg from Berlin,
  Who only 'tend to fits.

Dere vas Strobbich aus Westfalen
Who mofe all eart'ly ills
Mit concentrirter schinken juice,
Und Pumpernickel pills;
Und a bier-kur man from Munich,
Und a grape-curist from Rhein,
Und von who shkare tisease afay
Mit dose of Schlesier wein.

So dey meed in consooldation
Mit Doktor Winkeleck,
Who brackdise "renovation"
Mit sauerkraut und speck.
Und dat no man shouldt pe shlightet
Or treatet ash a tunce,
Dey 'greed to try deir systems
Oopon Breitmann all at vonce.

Dat ish, mit de excepdion,
Of gifin Schlesier wein;
For de remedy vas danger-full
On von who trink from Rhine.
Ash der teufel once declaret
Ven he taste it on a shpree,
Dat a man to trink soosh liquor
Moost a born Silesian pe.

So de all vent los at Breitmann,
  Und woonderfool to dell,
He coomed to his gesundheit,
  Und pooty soon cot vell,
Some hinted at *Natura*
  Mit de oldt *vis sanatrix*,
Boot each dokter shvore *he* cured him,
  Und de rest were Taugenix.

I know not vot der Breitmann
  More newly has pegun,
Boot dey say he dalks day-daily
  Mit Dana of de *Sun*.
Dey dalk in Deutsch togeder,
  Und volk say de ent vill pe
Philosopedal changes
  In de Union cavallrie.

Gott help de howlin safage!
  Gott help de Indi-an!
Shouldt Breitmann choin his forces
  Mit Sheneral Sheridan.
Und denn to sing his braises
  Acain I'll gife a lied—
Hier hat dis dale an ende
  Of Breitmann's philosopede.

A Ballad apout de Rowdies.

DE moon shines ofer de cloudlens,
Und de cloudts plow ofer de sea,
Und I vent to Coney Island,
Und I took mein Schatz mit me.
Mine Schatz, Katrina Bauer,
I gife her mein heart und vordt;
Boot ve tidn't know vot beoples
De Dampsschiff hafe cot on poard.

De preeze plowed cool und bleasant,
We looket at de town
Mit sonn-light on de shdeebles,
Und wetter fanes doornin round.
Ve sat on de deck in a gorner
Und dropled nopody dere,
Ven all aroundt oos de rowdies
Peginned to plackguard und schvear!

A voman mit a papy
Vas sittin in de blace;
Von tooket a chew tobacco
Und trowed it indo her vace.
De voman got coonvulshons,
De papy pegin to gry;
Und de rowdies shkreemed out a laffin,
Und saidt dat de fun vas "high."

Pimepy ve become some hoonger
  Katrina Baur und I,
I openet de lit of mine pasket,
  Und pringed out a cherry bie.
A cherry kooken mit pretzels,
  "How goot!" Katrina said,
Ven a rowdy snatched it from her,
  Und preaked it ofer mine het.

I dells him he pe a plackguart
  I gifed him a biece my mind,
I vouldt saidt it pefore a tousand,
  Mit der teufel himself pehind.
Den he knocks me down mit a sloong-shot,
  Und peats me plack and plue;
Und all de plackguards kick me,
  Dill I vainted, und dat ish drue.

De rich American beoples
  Don't know how de rowdies shtrike
Der poor hardt-workin Sherman,
  He knows it more ash he like.
If de Deutsche speakers und bapers
  Are sometimes too hard on dis land,
Shoost dink how de Deutsch kit driven
  Along by de rowdy's hand!

Wein Geist.

I STOOMPLED oud ov a dafern,
Berauscht mit a gallon of wein,
Und I rooshed along de Strassen,
Like a derriple Eberschwein.

Und like a lordly boar-big,
I doompled de soper folk;
Und I trowed a shtone droo a shdreed lamp,
Und bot' of de classes I proke.

Und a gal vent roonin' bast me.
Like a vild coose on de vings,
Boot I gatch her for all her skreechin,
Und giss her like afery dings.

Und denn mit an board und a shdore-box.
I blay de horse-viddle a biece,
Dill de neighbours shkreem "deat'!" und
"murder!"
Und holler aloudt "bolice?"

Und vhen der crim night wæchter
Says all of dis foon moost shtop,
I oop mit mein oombrella,
Und schlog him ober de kop.

I leaf him like tead on de bavemend,
  Und roosh droo a darklin' lane,
Dill moonlighd und tisdand musik,
  Pring me roundt to my soul again.

Und I sits all oonder de linden,
  De hearts-leaf linden dree;
Und I dink of de quick ge-vanisht lofe
  Dat vent like de vind from me.
Und I voonders in mine dipsy hood,
  If a damsel or dream vas she!

Dis life ish all a lindens
  Mit holes dat show de Plue;
Und pedween de finite pranches,
  Cooms Himmel light shinin troo.

De blaetter are raushlin' o'er me,
  Und efery leaf ish a fay,
Und dey vait dill de Windsbraut comet,
  To pear dem in Fall afay.

Und I look at a rock py de rifer,
  Vhere a stein ish of harpe form,
—Year dausend in, oud, it shtandet—
  Und nopody blays but de shtorm.

Here vonce on a dimes a vitches,
  Soom melodies here peginned,
De harpe ward all zu steine,
  Die melodie ward zu wind.

Und so mit dis tox-i-cation,
  Vitch hardens de outer Me;
Uber stein and schwein, de weine,
  Shdill harps oud a melodie.

Boot deeper de Ur-lied ringet,
  Ober stein und wein und svines,
Dill it endet vhere all peginnet,
  Und alles wird ewig zu eins,
In de dipsy, treamless sloomper
  Vhich units de Nichts und Seyns.

Breitmann in Politics.

I.--The Nomination.

VHEN ash de var vas ober,
  Und Beace her shnow-wice vings,
Vas vafin o'er de coondry
  (In shpods) like afery dings;
Und heroes vere revardtet,
  De beople all pegan
To say 'tvas shame dat nodings
  Vas done for Breitemann.

No man wised how id vas shtartet,
  Or where der fore shlog came,
Boot dey shveared it vas a cinder,
  Dereto a purnin shame:
"Dere is Schnitzerl in de Gustom-House—
  Potzblitz! can dis dings pe?—
Und Breitmann he hafe nodings:
  Vot sights is dis to see!

"Nod de virst ret cendt for Breitmann!
  Ish *dis* do pe de gry
On de man dat sacked de repels
  Und trinked dem high und dry?

By meine Seel' I shvears id,
  Und vot's more I deglares id's drue,
He vonce gleaned out a down in half an oor,
  Und shtripped id strumpf und shoe.

"He was shoost like Kœnig Etzel,
  Of whom de shdory dell,
Der Hun who go for de Romans
  Und gife dem shinin hell,
Only dis dat dey say no grass vouldt crow
  Vhere Etzel's horse had trot,
Und I really peliefe vere Breitmann go
  De hops shpring oop, bei Gott!"

If once you tie a dog loose,
  Dere ish more soon gets arount,
Und wenn dis vas shtartedt on Breitmann
  It was rings aroom be-foundt;
Dough *vhy* he *moost* hafe somedings
  Vas not by no mean glear,
Nor tid id, like Paulus' confersion,
  On de snap to all abbear!

Und, in facdt, Balthazar Bumchen
  Saidt he couldtent nicht blainly see
Vy a veller for gadderin riches
  Shood dus revartedt pe:

Der Breitmann own drei Houser,
  Mit a wein-handle in a stohr,
Dazu ein Lager-Wirthschaft,
  Und sonst was—somedings more.

Dis plasted plackguard none-sense
  Ve couldn't no means shtand,
From a narrow-mineted shvine's kopf,
  Of our nople captain grand :
Soosh low, goarse, betty *bornirtheit*
  A shentleman deplores ;
So ve called him *verfluchter Hundsfott*
  Und shmysed him out of toors.

So ve all dissolfed dat Breitmann
  Shouldt hafe a nomination
To go to de Legisladoor,
  To make some dings off de nation ;
Mit de helb of a Connedigut man,
  In whom ve hafe great hobes,
Who hat shange his boledics fivdeen dimes,
  Und derefore knew de robes.

II.—The Committee of Instruction.

DENN for our Insdructions Comedy
De ding vas protocollirt,
By Docktor Emsig Grubler,
Who in Jena vonce studiret;
Und for Breitmann his instrugtions
De Comedy tid say
Dat de All out-going from de Ones
Vash die first Moral Idée.

Und de segondt crate Moral Idée
Dat into him ve rings,
Vas dat government for avery man
Moost alfays do avery dings;
Und die next Idée do vitch his mindt
Esbecially ve gall,
Ish to do mitout a Bresident
Und no government at all.

Und die fourt Idée ve vish der Hans
Vouldt alfays keeb in fiew,
Ish to cooldifate die Peaudifool,
Likewise de Goot and Drue;
Und de form of dis oopright-hood
In proctise to present,
He most get our little pills all bassed
Mitout id's gostin a cent.

Und die fift' Idée—ash learnin
  Ish de cratest ding on eart,
And ash Shoopider der Vater
  To Minerfa gife ge-birt'—
Ve peg dat Breitmann oonto oos
  All pooblic tockuments
Vich he can grap or shteal vill sendt—
  Franked—mit his gompliments.

Die sechste crate Moral Idée—
  Since id fery vell ish known
Dat mind ish de resooldt of food,
  Ash der Moleschott has shown,
Und ash mind ish de highest form of Gott,
  As in Fichte dot' abbear—
He moost alfays go mit de barty
  Dat go for lager bier.

Now ash all dese instrugdions
  Vere showed to Misder Twine,
De Yangee boledician,
  He say dey vere fery fine :
Dey vere pesser ash goot, und almosdt nice—
  A tarnal tall concern ;—
Boot dey hafe some little trawpacks,
  Und in fagdt weren't worth a dern.

Boot yed, mit our bermission,
  If de shentlemans allow—
Here all der Shermans in de room
  Dake off deir hats und pow—
He vouldt gife our honored gandidate
  Some nodions of his own,
Hafing managed some elecdions
  Mit sookcess, as vell vas known.

Let him plow id all his *own* vay,
  He'd pet as sure as born,
Dat our mann vouldt not coom out of
  Der liddle endt der horn,
Mit his goot *proad* Sherman shoulders—
  Dis maket oos laugh, py shink!
So de comedy shtart for Breitmann's—
  Nota bene—afder a trink!

III.—Mr. Twine Explains Being "Sound Upon the Goose."

DERE in his crate corved oaken shtuhl
  Der Breitmann sot he:
He lookt shoost like de shiant
  In de Kinder hishdorie;
Und pefore him, on de tische,
  Vas—vhere man alfays foundt it—
Dwelf inches of goot lager,
  Mit a Bœmisch glass aroundt it.

De foorst vordt dat der Breitmann spoke
  He maked no sbeech or sign:
De next remark vas, "*Zapfet aus!*"—
  De dird vas, "*Schenket ein!*"
Vhen in coomed liddle Gottlieb
  Und Trina mit a shtock
Of allerbest Markgraefler wein—
  Dazu dwelf glaeser Bock.

Denn Misder Twine deglare dat he
  Vas happy to denounce
Dat as Copdain Breitmann suited oos
  Egsockdly do an ounce,

He vas ged de nomination,
  And need nod more eckshblain:
Der Breitmann dink in silence,
  And denn roar aloudt, CHAMPAGNE!

Den Mishder Twine, while trinken wein,
  Mitwhiles vent on do say,
Dat long insdruckdions in dis age
  Vere nod de dime of tay;
Und de only ding der Breitmann need
  To pe of any use
Vas shoost to dell to afery mans
  He's *soundt oopon der coose.*

Und ash dis little frase berhops
  Vas nod do oos bekannt,
He dakes de liberdy do make
  Dat ve shall oondershtand,
And vouldt tell a liddle shdory
  Vitch dook blace pefore de wars:
Here der Breitmann nod to Trina,
  Und she bass aroundt cigars.

"Id ish a longe dime, now here,
  In Bennsylvanien's Shtate,
All in der down of Horrisburg
  Dere rosed a vierce depate,

'Tween vamilies mit cooses,
  Und dose vhere none vere foundt—
If cooses might, by common law,
  Go squanderin aroundt?

"Dose who vere nod pe-gifted
  Mit gooses, und vere poor,
All shvear de law forbid dis crime,
  Py shings and cerdain sure;
But de coose-holders teklare a coose
  Greadt liberty tid need,
And to pen dem oop vas gruel,
  Und a mosdt oon-Christian teed.

"Und denn anoder party
  Idself tid soon refeal,
Of arisdograts who kepd no coose,
  Pecause 'twas not shendeel:
Tey tid not vish de splodderin geese
  Shouldt on deir pafcmends bass,
So dey shoined de anti-coosers,
  Or de oonder lower glass!"

Here Breitmann led his shdeam out:
  "Dis shdory goes to show
Dat in poledicks, ash lager,
  Virtus in medio.

De drecks ish ad de pottom—
  De skoom floads high inteed ;
Boot das bier ish in de mittle,
  Says an goot old Sherman lied.

" Und shoost apout elegdion-dimes
  De scoom und drecks, ve see,
Have a pully Wahl-verwandtschaft,
  Or election-sympathie."
" Dis is very vine," says Misder Twine,
  " Vot here you indroduce :
Mit your bermission, I'll grack on
  Mit my shdory of de coose.

" A gandertate for sheriff
  De coose-beholders run,
Who shvear de coose de noblest dings
  Vot valk peneat de sun ;
For de cooses safe de Capidol
  In Rome long dimes ago,
Und Horrisburg need safin
  Mighty pad, ash all do know.

" Acainsd dis mighdy Goose-man
  Anoder veller rose,
Who keepedt himself ungommon shtill
  Ven oders came to plows ;

Und if any ask how 'twas he shtoodt,
His vriends wouldt vink so loose,
Und visper ash dey dapped deir nose :
' *He's soundt oopon de coose !*

" ' He's O. K. oopon de soobject ;
Shoost pet your pile on dat ;
On dis bartik'ler quesdion
He intends to coot it fat.'
So de veller cot elegded
Pefore de beople foundt
On *vitch* site of der coose it vas
He shtick so awful soundt.

" Dis shdory's all I hafe to dell,"
Says Misder Hiram Twine ;
" Und I advise Herr Breitmann
Shoost to vight id on dis line."
De volk who of dese boledics
Would oder shapters read,
Moost waiten for de segondt pardt
Of dis here Breitmann's Lied.

IV.—How Breitmann and Schmit were Reported to be Log-Rolling.

Id happenet in de yar of crace,
  Ven all dese dings pegan,
Dat Mishder Schmit, de shap who rooned
Acainsd der Breitemann,
  Vas a man who look like Mishder Twine
So moosh dat beoples say
  Dey pliefe dey moost ge-brudert pe—
Gott weiss in vot a vay!

Und id vas also moosh be-marked—
  Vitch look shoost like a bruder—
Dat ven Twine vas vork on any side
  Der Schmit vas on de oder:
A fery gommon dodge ish dis
  Mit de arisdocracie;
So dat votefer cardt toorns oop,
  Id's game for de familie!

Nun, goot! Howefer dis mighdt pe,
  'Tvas cerdain on dis hit
Der Twine vas do his teufelest
  To euchre Mishder Schmit;
Und Schmit, I criefe to say, exglaimed:
  "Goll darn me for a fool,
But I'll smash old Dutch to cholera fits
  And rake the eternal pool!"

So dey cot some liddle ledders,
  Ash brifate ash could pe,
Vitch Breitmann writed long agone
  To friendts in Germany ;
Und dey brinted dem in efery vay
  To make de beoples laugh,
Und comment on dem in de shtyle
  Dat "sports" call "slasher-gaff."

Dere to—as vash known py shoodshment
  Und glearly ascerdaind,
Dat Breitmann hafe lossed money
  Py a valse und schwindlin friend—
So dey roon it troo de newsbapers,
  Und shbeech do make pegan,
Dat *Breitmann* shtole de gelt himself
  Und rop der oder man.

Boot de ding dat jam de hardest
  On de men dat bull de vires,
Und showed dat Captain Breitmann
  Shtood pedween dwo heafy vires,
Vas, pecause he vas a soldier—
  Von could see id at a clanse—
Dey had pud him in a tisdrigt
  Vhere he hadn't half a shanse.

For ash de pold solidaten
  Ish more prafe ash oder mans,
Dey moost lead de hope verloren
  Und pattle in de vans;
Und ash defeat ish honoraple
  To men in honor shtrict,
Dey honor dem py puttin em
  Vhere dey're cerdain to pe licked.

Boot dis dimes it shlopped over,
  Tvas de dird or secondt heat
Dat a soldier in dis tisdrigt
  Had been poot oop und beat:
So de Plue Goats dink it over
  Und go quietly to vork:
De bow ven too moosh aufgespannt
  Vlies packward mit a yerk.

Now Mishder Twine deglaret on dis
  De ding seemed doubtenfull,
Boot mitout delay he dook de horns
  So poldly py de bull,
Und shpread de shdory eferyvhere,
  Dill folk to pliefe pegan,
Dat Mishder Schmit had *sold de vight*
  Unto der Breitemann!

He fix de liddle tedails—
  How moosh der Schmit hafe got
For sellin out his barty
  To let Breitmann haul de pot;
Und he showed a brifate ledder
  From Breitemann to Schmit,
Vhere he bromise him for Congress
  If he shoost let oop a bit.

Der Twine vas writet dis ledder;
  For der Copitain Breitemann
Vould nefer hafe shtood soosh hoompoogks
  Since virst his life pegan;
He hat tone some rough dings in der war,
  In de ploonder-und-morder line,
Boot vas hoockelperry-persimmoned
  Mit dese boledics of Twine.

Howefer, dis ledder vorket foorst-rade—
  Mit de Merigans pest of all,
For dey mostly dinked it de naturalest ding
  As efer couldt pefall;
For to sheat von's own gonstituents
  Ish de pest mofe in de came,
Und dey nefer sooposed a Dootchman
  Hafe de sense to do de same

V.—How they held the Mass Meeting.

DERE's nodings in dis vorldt so pad,
 Ash all oov us may learn,
Boot may shange from dark to lighthood,
 If loock should dake a doorn ;
So it happenet mit Breitmann,
 Who in shpite of sin und Schmit,
Gontrified ad shoost dis yooncture
 Do make a glucky hit.

Dey hat sendet out some plackarts
 To de Deutsche buergers all
(N. B.—Dish ish not mean *plackarts*,
 Boot de pills dey shtick on de vall),
To say dat a Massenversammlung—
 Or a meeding of all de masses—
Vould be held in de Arbeiter-Halle,
 To consisd of de Sharman classes.

Now dey gife de brintin of de pills
 To a new gekommene man,
Who dinked dat Demokratisch
 Vas de same ash Repooblican :
Gott in Himmel weiss where he hid himself
 On dish free Coloompian shore
Dat he scaped de naturalizationisds,
 Und hadn't found out pefore.

Boot to dis Deutsche brinter,
  De only tifference he
Petween Repooblicanish
  Und Demokratisch tid sec,
Vas dat von vash dwo ledders longer;
  So he dook shoost vot seem pat
To make de poster handsome—
  Likewise a liddle fat.

How ofden in dis buzzlin life
  Small grubs grows oop to vings!
How ofden shoost from moostard seet
  A virst-glass pusiness shprings!
Vant klein komt men tot't groote,
  Ash de Hollanders hafe said:
Mit dese dwo ledders Breitemann
  Caved in der Schmitsy's head.

VI.—Breitmann's Great Speech.

DIS tale dat Schmit hafe *seu de vight*
Cot so much put apout
Dat many of his beoples vere
In fery tupious toubt;
'Pove all, dose who were on de make,
And easy change deir lodge,
Und, pein awfool smart demselfs,
Pelieve in every dodge.

Vhen de meeding vas gesempled,
Und dey found no Schmit vas dere,
Dey looket at von anoder
Mit a *ganz* erstaunished air;
But dey *saw it* glear as taylight,
Und around a vink dere ran,
Ven pefore dem rose de shiant form
Of Copitain Breitemann!

Den Breitemann vent los at dem:
" He could nichts well exbress
De rapdure dat besqueezed his hearts—
De wonnevol hoppiness—
To meed in friendlich council
And glasp de hand of dose
Who had peen mit most oonreason
Und unkindtly galled his foes.

"Berhaps o'er all dis shmilin eart'—
He vould say it dere and den—
Soosh shpecdagles couldt nod pe seen
Of soosh imbartial men,
So tefoid of pase sospicion,
So apove all betty dricks,
Ash to gome und lisden vairly
To a voe in poledicks;

"Dat ish to say, a so-galled voe—
For he feeled id in his soul
Dat de *brinciples* vitch mofed dem
Vere de same oopon de whole;
But he lack a vord to exbress dem
In manners opportunes—"
Here a veller in de gallery
Gry oud, oonkindly, "Shpoons!"

Und dere der Breitmann goppled him:
"If *shpoons* our modifes pe,
Dere's not a man pefore oos
Who lossed a shpoon by me:
Far rader had I gife you all
A shpoons to eaten mit,
Und I hope to get a ladle for
Mine friendt, der Mishder Schmit."

Dis fetch das Haus like doonder—
  It raised der teufel's dust,
Und for sefen-lefen minudes
  Dey ooplauded on a bust;
Und de blokes dat dinked of hedgin
  Saw a ring as round as O;
So dey boked eash oder in de rips,
  Und said, "I dold you so!"

For dis d'lusion to de ladle
  Vas as glear ash city milk,
Und drawd it on de beoples
  So vine ash flossen silk,
Dat Hans und Schmit vere rollin locks,
  Und de locks were ready cut;
Only Breitmann hafe de liddle end,
  Und Schmitsy dake de butt!

Den Breitemann he crack onward:
  "If any 'lightened man
Will seeken in his Bibel,
  He'll find dat a publican
Is a barty ash sells lager;
  Und das ding is ferry blain,
Dat a *re*-publican ish von
  Who sells id 'gain und 'gain.

“Now since dat I sells lager,
  I gant agreen mit
De demprance brinciples I hear
  Distriputet to Schmit;
Boot dis I dells you vairly,
  Und no one to teseife—
If I were Schmit, I'd pliefen
  Shoost vot der Schmit peliefe.

“And to mine Sherman, liperal friends
  I might mention in dis shpot
Dat I hear an oonfoundet rumor
  Dat der Schmit peliefe in Gott;
Und also dat he coes to shoorsh—
  Mit a prayer-book for salfadion:
I vould not for die welt say dings
  To hoort his repudadion.

“Und nodin is more likely
  Dat it all a shlander pe,
So also de rumor dat ven young
  He shtoody divinidy:
I myself, ash a publican,
  Moost pe a sinner by fate,
Und in dis sense I denounce myself
  Ash Re-publi-candidate!

" Und dat ve may meed in gommon,
   I declare here in dis hall—
Und I shvears mineself to hold to it,
   Fotefer may pefall—
Dat any man who gifes me his fote—
   Votevefer his boledicks pe—
Shall alfays pe regartet
   Ash bolidigal friendt py me."

(Dis voonderfol condescension
   Pring down drementous applause,
Und dose who catch de nodion
   Gife most derriple hooraws;
Eshbecially some Amerigans
   Ash vas shtandin near de door,
Und who in all deir leben long
   Nefer heard so moosh sense pefore.)

" Dese ish de brincibles I holts,
   And dose in vitch I run:
Dey ish fixed firm and immutaple
   Ash te course of de 'ternal sun:
Boot if you ton't abbrove of dem—
   Blease nodice vot I say—
I shall only pe too happy
   To alder dem right afay.

"Und unto my Demogratic friendts
I vould very glearly shtate—
Since dis useless mit oop-geclearéd minds
To hold a long depate—
Dat dere's no man in de cidy
Dat sells besser liquor ash I,
Und I shtand de treadts *free-gradis*
Vhenefer mine friendts ish try.

"*Ad finem*—in de ende—
I moost mendion do you all,
Dat a dootzen parrels of lager bier
Ish a-gomin to dis hall:
Dere ish none of mine own barty here,
Boot we'll do mitout deir helfs;
Und I kess, on de whole, 'twill pe shoost so goot,
If ve trink it all ourselfs."

Soosh drementous up-loudation
Pefore was nefer seen,
Ash dey shvored dat Copitan Breitmann
Vas a brick-pat, and no sardine;
Und dey trinked demselfs besoffen,
Sayin, "Hope you wird sookceed!"—
De nexter theil will pe de ent
Of dis historisch lied.

VII.—The Author Asserts the Vast Intellectual Superiority of Germans to Americans.

DERE's a liddle fact in hishdory
Vich few hafe oonderstand—
Dat de Deutschers are, *de jure*,
De owners of dis land;
Und I brides mineself unspeakbarly
Dat I foorst make be-known
De primordial cause dat Columpus
Vas derivet from Cologne;

For ash his name vas Colon,
It fisibly does shine
Dat his elders are geboren been
In Co-logne on der Rhein;
Und Colonia pein a colony,
It sehr bemarkbar ist
Dat Columbus in America
Was der firster colonist.

Und ash Columbus is a tofe,
Id is wort de drople to mark
Dat a bidgeon foorst tiscofered land
A-vlyin from de ark;
Und shtill wider—in de peginnin,
Mitout de leastest toubt,
A tofe vas vly ofer de wassers
Und pring de vorldt herout.

Ash mine goot oldt teacher der Kreutzer
　To me tid often shbeak,
De mythus of name rebeats idself
　(Vich ve see in his *Symbolik*);
So also de name America,
　If ve a liddle look,
Vas coom from de oldt King Emerich
　In de Deutsche *Heldenbuch*.

Und id vas from dat very *Heldenbuch*—
　How voonderful id run!—
Dat I shdole de "Song of Hildebrand,
　Or der Vater und der Son,"
Und dishtripute it to Breitmann,
　For a reason vitch now ish plain,
Dat dis Sagen-Cyclus, full-endet,
　Pring me round to der Hans again!

Dese laws of un-endly un-wigglin
　Ish so teep und broad und tall
Dat nopody boot a Deutscher
　Have a het to versteh dem at all;
Und should I write mine dinks all oud,
　I ton't peliefe, indeed,
Dat I mineself vould versteh de half
　Of dis here Breitmannslied.

Ash de Hegel say of his system,
  Dat only von mans knew
Vot der teufel id meandt, und *he* could't tell;
  Und der Jean Paul Richter too,
Who said, " Gott knows I meant somedings
  When foorst dis buch I writ,
Boot Gott only wise vot de buch means now,
  Vor I have vergotten it."

And all of dis be-wises
  So blain ash de face on your nose,
Dat der Deutscher hafe efen more intellects,
  Dan he himself soopose;
Und his tifference mit de over-again vorldt,
  Ash I really do soospect,
Ish dat oder volk hafe more *soopose*,
  Und lesser intellect.

Yet coprightly I gonfess it—
  Mitout ashkin vhy or vhence—
Dere ish also dimes vhen Amerigans
  Hafe ge-shown sharp-pointed sense;
Und a fery outsigned example
  Of genius in dis line
Vas dishblayed in dis elegdion
  Py Mishder Hiram Twine.

VIII.—Showing How Mr. Hiram Twine "Played off" on Smith.

VIDE LICET : Dere vas a fillage
Whose vode alone vouldt pe
Apout enoof to elegdt a man,
Und gife a mayority;
So de von who couldt scoop dis seddlement
Vould make a pully hit;
Boot dough dey vere Deutschers, von und all,
Dey all go von on Schmit.

Now it happenet to gome to bass
Dat in dis liddle town
De Deutsch vas all exshpegdin
Dat Mishder Schmit coom down,
His brinciples to fore-setzen
Und his ideés to deach,
(Dat is, fix oop de brifate pargains)
Und telifer a pooblic sbeech.

Now Twine vas a gyrotwistive cuss,
Ash blainly ish peen shown,
Und vas alfays an out-findin
Votefer might pe known ;
Und mit some of his circumswindles
He fix de matter so
Dat he'd pe himself at dis meetin
And see how dings vas go.

Oh shtrangely in dis leben
  De dings kits vorked apout!
Oh voonderly Fortuna
  Makes toorn us insite out!
Oh sinkular de luck-wheel rolls!
  Dis liddle meeding dere
Fixt Twine *ad perpendiculum*—
  Shoost suit him to a hair!

Now it hoppenit on dis efenin
  De Deutschers, von und all,
Vere avaitin mit impatience
  De openin of de ball;
Und de shates of nite vere fallin
  Und de shdars begin to plink,
Und dey vish dat Schmit vouldt hoorry,
  For d'vas dime to dake a trink.

Dey hear some hoofs a-dramplin,
  Und dey saw, und dinked dey knowed,
Der bretty greature coomin,
  On his horse along de road;
Und ash he ride town in-ward
  De likeness vas so plain
Dey donnered out, "Hooray for Schmit!"
  Enough to make it rain.

Der Twine vas shtart like plazes;
  Boot oopshtarted too his wit,
Und he dinks, "Great Turnips ! what if I
  Could bass for Colonel Schmit ?
Gaul dern my heels ! *I'll do it,*
  Und go the total swine !
Oh, Soap-balls ! what a chance !" said dis
  Dissembulatin Twine.

Den 'twas "Willkomm ! willkomm, Mishder
    Schmit !"
  Ringsroom on efery site ;
Und "First-rate ! How dy-do yourself ?"
  Der Hiram Twine replied.
Dey ashk him, "Come und dake a trink ?"
  But dey find it mighdy queer
Ven Twine informs dem none boot hogs
  Vould trink dat shtinkin bier ;

Dat all lager vas nodings boot boison ;
  Und ash for Sherman wein,
He dinks it vas erfounden
  Exshbressly for Sherman schwein ;
Dat he himself vas a demperanceler—
  Dat he gloria in de name ;
Und atfise dem all, for tecency's sake,
  To go und do de same.

Dese bemarks among de Deutschers
  Vere apout ash vell receife
Ash a cats in a game of den-bins,
  Ash you may of coorse peliefe :
De heat of de reception
  Vent down a dootzen tegrees,
Und in place of hurraws dere vas only heardt
  De rooslin of de drees.

Und so in solemn stille
  Dey scorched him to de hall,
Vhere he maket de oradion
  Vitch vas so moosh to blease dem all ;
Und dis vay he pegin it :
  "Pefore I furder go,
I vish dat my obinions
  You puddin-het Dootch should know.

"Und ere I norate to you,
  I think it only fair
We should oonderstand each other
  Prezactly, chunk and square.
Dere are boints on vhich ve tisagree,
  And I will plank de facts—
I don't go round slanganderin
  My friendts pehind deir packs.

" So I beg you dake it easy
If on de raw I touch,
Vhen I say I can't apide de sound
Of your groontin, shi-shing Dutch.
Should I in the Legisladure
As your slumgullion shtand,
I'll have a bill forbidding Dutch
Troo all dis 'versal land.

"Should a husband talk it to his frau,
To deat' he should pe led;
If a mutter breat' it to her shild,
I'd bunch her in de head;
Und I'm sure dat none vill atfocate
Ids use in public schools,
Oonless dey're peastly, nashdy, prutal,
Sauerkraut-eatin vools.

Here Mishder Twine, to gadder breat,
Shoost make a liddle pause,
Und see sechs hundert gapin eyes,
Sechs hundert shdarin chaws,
Dey shtanden erstarrt like frozen;
Von faindly dried to hiss;
Und von set: "Ish it shleeps I'm treamin?
Gottausend! vat ish dis?"

Twine keptet von eye on de vindow,
  Boot poldly went ahet:
" Of your oder shtinkin hobits
  No vordt needt hier pe set.
Shtop goozlin bier—shtop shmokin bipes—
  Shtop rootin in de mire ;
Und shoost *un-Dutchify* yourselfs :
  Dat's all dat I require."

Und *denn* dere coomed a shindy
  Ash if de shky hat trop:
" Trow him mit ecks, py doonder !
  Go shlog him on de kop !
Hei ! Shoot him mit a powie-knifes ;
  Go for him, ganz and gar !
Shoost tar him mit some fedders !
  Led's fedder him mit tar !"

Sooch a teufel's row of furie
  Vas nefer oop-kickt before:
Soom roosh to on-climb de blatform—
  Soom hoory to fasten te toor :
Von veller vired his refolfer,
  Boot de pullet missed her mark:
She coot de cort of de shandelier :
  It vell, und de hall vas tark !

Oh vell was it for Hiram Twine
  Dat nimply he couldt shoomp;
Und vell dat he light on a misthauf,
  Und nefer feel de boomp;
Und vell for him dat his goot cray horse
  Shtood sattled shoost outside;
Und vell dat in an augenblick
  He vas off on a teufel's ride.

Bang ! bang ! de sharp pistolen shots
  Vent pipin py his ear,
Boot he tortled oop de barrick road
  Like any mountain deer :
Dey trowed der Hiram Twine mit shteins,
  But dey only could be-mark
Von climpse of his vhite obercoadt,
  Und a clotterin in de tark.

So dey all versembled togeder,
  Ein ander to sprechen mit,
Und allow dat sooch a rede
  Dey nefer exshpegd from Schmit—
Dat he vas a foorst-glass plackguard,
  And so pig a Lump ash ran ;
So, *nemine contradicente,*
  Dey vented for Breitemann.

Und 'twas annerthalb yar dereafter
  Before der Schmit vas know
Vot maket dis rural fillage
  Go pack oopon him so;
Und he schvored at de Dootch more schlimmer
  Ash Hiram Twine had tone.
Nota bene: He tid it in earnesht,
  Vhile der Hiram's vas pusiness fun.

Boot vhen Breitmann heard de shdory
  How de fillage hat peen dricked,
He shvore bei Leib und Leben
  He'd rader hafe been licked
Dan pe helpet bei soosh shumgoozlin;
  Und 'twas petter to pe a schwein
Dan a schwindlin honeyfooglin shnake,
  Like dat lyin Yankee Twine.

Und pegot so heafy disgoosted
  Mit de boledicks of dis land
Dat his friendts couldn't barely keep him
  From trowin oop his hand, [poot;
Vhen he helt shtraidt flush, mit an ace in his
  Vich phrase ish all de same,
In de science of de pokerology,
  Ash if he got de game.

So Breitmann cot elegtet,
  Py vollowin de vay
Dey manage de elegdions
  Unto dis fery day;
Vitch shows de Deutsch *Dummehrlichkeit*,
  Also de Yankee " wit:"
Das ist das Abenteuer
  How Breitmann lick der Schmit

Hans Breitmann In Church.

With Other New Ballads.

BY CHARLES G. LELAND.

AUTHOR OF "HANS BREITMANN'S PARTY, AND OTHER NEW BALLADS," "HANS BREITMANN ABOUT TOWN," ETC., ETC.

Third Series of the Breitmann Ballads.

PHILADELPHIA:
T. B. PETERSON & BROTHERS;
306 CHESTNUT STREET.

Contents.

Editor's Preface.

THE Editor has pleasure in being at length enabled to publish a new and "Third Series" of the "Breitmann Ballads," and does so, in the hope that these latest poems will sustain the high reputation gained for the author by his previous labours in the same field of poetry.

As regards some of the points and incidents of the poems contained in this volume, the following remarks may not be inappropriate.

The ballad, "Breitmann's Going to Church," is based on a real occurrence. A certain colonel, with his men, did really, during the war, go to a church in or near Nashville, and, as the saying is, "kicked up the devil, and broke things," to such an extent, that a serious reprimand from the colonel's superior officer was the result. The fact is guaranteed by Mr. Leland, who heard the offender complain of the "cruel and heartless stretch of military authority." As regards the firing into the guerilla ball-room, it took place near Murfreesboro', on the night of Feb. 10 or 11, 1865; and on the next day, Mr. Leland was at a house where one of the wounded lay. On the same night a Federal picket was shot dead near Lavergne; and the next night a detachment of cavalry was sent off from General Van Cleve's quarters, the officer in command coming in, while the author was talking with the general, for final orders. They rode twenty miles that night, attacked a body of guerillas, captured a number, and brought them back as prisoners early next day. The same day Mr. Leland, with a small cavalry escort and a few friends, went out into the country; and during the ride one or two curious incidents occurred, illustrating the extraordinary fidelity of the blacks to the Federal soldiers.

The explanation of the poem entitled, "The First Edition of Breitmann," is as follows: It was not long after the war that a friend of the writer's to whom "The Breitmann Ballads" had been sent in MSS., and who had frequently urged the former to

have them published, resolved to secure, at least, a small private edition, though at his own expense. Unfortunately the printers quarrelled about the MSS., and, as the writer understood, the entire concern broke up in a row in consequence. And, in fact, when we reflect on the amount of fierce attack and recrimination which this unpretending and peaceful little volume elicited in England after the appearance of the fifth English edition, the injury which it sustained from garbled and falsified editions in that country, and an unauthorised Australian reprint, it would really seem as if this first edition, which "died a borning," had been typical of the stormy path to which the work was predestined.

"I Gili Romaneskro," a gipsy ballad, was written both in the original and translation—that is to say, in the German gipsy and German English dialects—to cast a new light on the many-sided Bohemianism of Herr Breitmann. "Steinli von Slang" is simply a lay or a ballad amplified to a romance. The lines "To a Friend Studying German," may be, we believe, appropriately enough addressed to any lady or gentleman employed in mastering the mighty and mysterious head of the Teutonic branches. For the author having been assured that great numbers of this book were bought to present, in the way of jest, to friends devoted to the study of German, it occurred to him that a poem devoted to this subject would not be unacceptable.

Breitmann's Going to Church.

" *Vides igitur, Collega carissime, visitationem canonicam esse rem haud ita periculosam, sed valde amœnam, si modo vinum, groggio, et cibi praesto sunt.*"

[*Novissimæ Epistolæ Obscurorum Virorum. Berlini, F. Berggold*, 1869. *Epistola* xxiii. *p.* 63.]

D'VAS near de State of Nashfille,
In de town of Tennessee,
Der Breitmann vonce vas quarderd
Mit all his cavallrie.
Der Sheneral kept him glose in camp,
He vouldn't let dem go,
Dey couldn't shdeal de first plack hen,
Or make de red cock crow.

Und virst der Breitmann vildly shmiled,
Und denn he madly shvore:
" Crate h—l mit shpoons und shinsherbread!
Can dis pe makin war?
Verdammt pe all der discipline;
Verdammt der Sheneràl;
Vere I vonce on de road, his will
Were Wurst mir und egâl.

"Oh vhere ish all de plazin roofs
  Dat claddened vonce mine eyes,
Und vhere de crand blantaschions
  Vhere ve gaddered many a brize?
Und vhere de plasted shpies ve hung
  A howlin loud mit fear;
Und vhere de rascal push-whackers
  Ve shashed like vritened deer.

"De roofs are shtandin fast und firm
  Mit repels blottin oonder;
De crand blantaschions lie round loose
  For Morgan's men to ploonder;
De shbies go valkin out und in,
  Ash sassy ash can pe,
Und in de voods de push-whackers
  Are makin foon of me!

"O, vere I on my schimmel grey,
  Mein sabre in mein hand,
Dey should drack me py de ruins
  Of de houses troo de land.
Dey should drack me py de puzzards
  High sailen ofer head,
A vollowin der Breitmann's trail,
  To claw de repel dead."

Outspoke der bold Von Stossenheim,
  Who had théories of Gott:
" O Breitmann dis ish shoodgement on
  De vays dat you hafe trot.
You only lifes to joy yourself,
  Yet you yourself moost say
Dat self-development requires
  De réligiös Idée."

Dey set dem down und argued it,
  Like Deutschers vree from fear,
Dill dey schmoke ten pfounds of Knaster
  Und drinked drei fass of bier.
Der Breitmann go py Schopenhauer,
  Boot Veit he had him denn,
For he dook him on de angles
  Of de moral oxygen.

Der Breitmann 'low dat 'pentence
  Ish known in afery glime,
Und dat to grin und bear it
  Vas healty und sooplime.
" For mine Sout Sherman Catoliks
  Id vas pe goot I know,
Likevise dem Nordland Luterans,
  If vonce to shoorsh dey go.

"Boot how vas id mit oders
Who dinks philosophie?
I don't begreif de matter—"
Said Stossenheim: "Denn see
De more dat Shoorsh disgoostet you,
Und make despise und bain,
De crater merid ish to go,
Und de crater ish your gain.

"I know a liddle shoorsh mineself
Oopon de Bole Jack road;
(De rebs vonce shot dree Federals dere
Ash into shoorsh dey goed.)
Dere you might make a bilcrimage,
Und do it in a tay:—
Gott only knows vot dings you might
Bick oop, oopon de vay."

Den oop dere shpoke a contrapand,
Vas at de tent id's toor:
"Dere's twenty bar'ls of whisky hid
In dat tabernacle—shore!
A rebel he done gone and put
It in de cellar true;
No libin man dat secret knows
'Cept only me an' you."

Der Stossenheim he grossed himself
   Und knelt peside de fence,
Und gried: " O Coptain Breitmann, see,
   Die finger Providence."
Der Breitmann droed his hat afay:
   Says he, " Pe't hit or miss,
I'fe heard of miragles pefore,
   Boot none so hunk ash dis.

" Wohl auf, mine pully cafaliers,
   Ve'll ride to shoorsh to-day!
Each man ash hasn't cot a horse,
   Moost shteal von, rite afay.
Dere's a raw, green corps from Michigan,
   Mit horses on de loose;
You men ash vants some hoof-iróns,
   Look out und crip deir shoes!"

All brooshed und fixed, de cavallrie
   Rode out py moonen-shine;
De cotten fields in shimmerin light
   Lay white ash elfenbein.
Dey heared a shot close py Lavergne,
   Und men who rode afay.
In de road a-velterin in his ploot
   A Federal picket lay.

Und all dat he hafe dimes to say:
"Vhile shtandin at my post,
De guerillas got first shot at me;"
Und so gafe oop de ghost.
Den a contrapand, who helt his head,
Said: "Sah—dose grillers all,
Is only half a mile from hyar,
A dancin at a pall."

Der Breitmann shpoke, und brummed it out
Ash if his heart tid schvell,
"I'll gife dem music at dat pall
Vill tantz dem indo hell!"
Hei!—arrow-fast—a teufel's ride!
De plack man led de vay;
Dey reach de house—dey see de lights—
Dey heard de fiddle blay.

Dey nefer vaited for a word,
Boot galloped from de gloom,
Und *bang!*—a hoonderd carpine shots
Dey fired into de room.
Oop vent de groans of vountet men,
De fittlin died avay;
Boot some of dem vere tead before
De music ceased to blay.

Den crack und smack coom scatterin shots
Troo vindow und troo door,
Boot bang und clang de Germans gife
Anoder volley more.
"Dere—let 'em shlide. Right file, to shoorsh!"
Aloudt de orders ran.
"I kess I paid dem for dat shot!"
Shpeak grim der Breitemann.

All rosen red de mornin fair
Shone gaily o'er de hill,
All violet plue de shky crew teep
In rifer, pond und rill.
All cloudy grey de limeshtone rocks
Coom oop troo dimmerin wood;
All shnowy vite in mornin light
De shoorsh pefore dem shtood.

"Now loudet vell de Organ oop,
To drill mit solemn fear;
Und ring alsò dat Lumpenglock,
To pring de beoples here.
Und if it prings guerillas down,
Ve'll gife dem, py de Lord!
De low mass of de sabre, und
De high mass of de cord!

"Du Eberlé aus Freiburg,
Du bist ein Musikant.
Top-sawyer on de counter-point
Und buster in discánt,
To dee de soul of music
All innerly ish known,
Du canst mit might fullenden
De art of orgel-ton.

"Derefore a Miserére
Vilt dou, be-ghostet, spiel;
Und vake re-raiséd yearnin,
Alsó a holy feel :—
Pe referent, men—remember
Dis ish a Gotteshaus—
Du, Conrad,—go along de aisles,
Und schenk de whisky aus!"

Dey blay crate dings from Mozart,
Beethoven und Méhul,
Mit chorals of Sebastian Bach,
Sooplime und peaudiful.
Der Breitmann feel like holy saints,
De tears roon down his fuss,
Und he sopped out: "Gott verdammich—dis
Ist wahres Kunstgenuss!"

Der Eberlé blayed oop so high
He make de rafters ring.
Der Eberlé blayed lower, und
Ve heardt der Breitmann sing,
Like a dronin wind in piney woods,
Like a nightly moanin sea,
Ash he dinked on Sonntags long agone
Vhen a poy in Germany.

Und louder und mit louder tone
High oop de orgel blowed,
Und plentifuller efer yet
Around de whisky goed.
Dey singed ash if mit singin dey
Might indo Himmel win:—
I dink in all dis land soosh shprees
Ash yet hafe nefer peen.

Vhen in de Abendsonnenschein,
Mit doost-cloudts troo de door,
All plack ash night in goldnen lighdt
Dere shtood ein schwartzer Mohr.
Dat contrapand so wild und weh,
Mit eye-palls glarin round,
Und cried: "For Gott's sake, hoory oop!
De reps ish gomin down!"

Und vhile he yet vas shpeakin,
  A far-off soundt pegan,
Down rollin from de moundain,
  Of many a ridersmann.
Und vhile de waves of musik
  Vere rollin o'er deir heads,
Dey heard a foice a schkreemin:
  "Pile out of thar, you Feds!

"For we uns ar' a comin
  For to guv to you uns fits,
And knock you into brimstun,
  And blast you all to bits—"
Boot ere it done ids shpeakin
  Dere vas order in de band,
Ash Breitmann, mit an awefool stim
  Out-dondered his gommand.

Und ash fisch-hawk at a mackarel
  Doth make a splurgin flung,
Und ash eagles dab de fisch-hawks
  Ash if de gods were young;
So from all de doors und vindows,
  Like shpiders down deir webs,
De Dootch went at deir horses,
  Und de horses at de rebs.

Crate shplendors of de treadful
   Vere in dat pattle rush;
Crate vights mit swordt und carpine
   Py efery fence and bush;
Ash panters vight mit crislies
   In famished morder fits—
For de rebs vere mad ash boison,
   Und de Dootch ver droonk as blitz.

Yet vild ash vas dis pattle,
   So quickly vas it o'er:—
O vhy moost I forefer
   Pestain mine page mit gore
Py liddle und py liddle,
   Dey drawed demselfs afay;
Oft toornin round to vighten,
   Like booffaloes at bay.

De scatterin shots grew fewer,
   De scatterin gries more shlow;
Und furder troo de forest
   Ve heared dem vainter crow.
Ve gife von shout—"*Victoria!*"
   Und den der Breitmann said,
Ash he wiped his ploody sabre,
   "Now, poys, count oop your dead!"

O small had peen our shoutin
  For shoy, if ve had known,
Dat de Stossenheim im oaken Wald
  Lay dyin all alone;
Vhile his oldt white horse mit droopin het
  Look dumbly on him down,
Ash if he dinked, "Vy lyest dou here
  Vhile fightin's goin on?"

Und dreams coom o'er de soldier,
  Slow dyin on de eart,
Of a Schloss afar in Baden,
  Of his mutter, und nople birt—
Of poverty und sorrow
  Vhich drofe him like de wind—
Und he sighed: "Ach weh, for de lofed ones
  Who wait so far pehind!

"Wohl auf, my soul o'er de moundains!
  Wohl auf—well ofer de sea!
Dere's a frau dat sits in de Odenwald,
  Und shpins, und dinks of me.
Dere's a shild ash blays in de greenin grass,
  Und sings a liddle hymn,
Und learns to shpeak a fader's name
  Dat she nefer will shpeak to him.

"But mordal life ends shortly,
  Und Heafen's life is long—
Wo bist du, Breitmann?—glaub'es—
  Gott suffers no ding wrong.
Now I die like a Christian soldier;
  My head oopon my sword:—
In nomine Domine!"
  Vas Stossenheim his word.

O, dere vas bitter wailen
  Vhen Stossenheim vas found,
Efen from dose dere lyin
  Fast dyin on de grount.
Boot time vas short for vaiten,
  De shades vere gadderin dim;
Und I nefer shall forget it,
  De hour ve puried him.

De tramp of horse und soldiers
  Vas all de funeral knell,
De ring of sporn und carpine
  Vas all de sacrin bell.
Mit hoontin knife und sabre
  Dey digged de grave a span;
From German eyes blue gleamin
  De holy water ran.

Mit moss-grown shticks und bark-thong
  De plessed cross ve made,
Und put it vhere de soldier's head
  Toward Germany vas laid.
Dat grave is lost mid dead leafs,
  De cross is gone afay,
Boot Gott will find der reiter
  Oopon de Youngest Day.

Und dinkin of de fightin,
  Und dinkin of de dead,
Und dinkin of de Organ,
  To Nashville Breitmann led.
Boot long dat rough oldt Hanserl
  Vas ernsthaft, grim und kalt,
Shtill dinkin of de heart's friend,
  He'd left im gruenen Wald.

De verses of dis boem
  In Heidelberg I write.
De night is dark around me,
  De shtars apove are bright.
Studenten in den Gassen
  Make singen many a song,
Ach Faderland!—wie bist du weit!
  Ach Zeit!—wie bist du lang!

The First Edition of Breitmann.

Showing how and why it was that it never appeared.

> *"Uns ist in alten Maeren,*
> *Wunders viel geseit,*
> *Von Helden lobebaeren,*
> *Von grosser Arebeit,*
> *Von Festen und Hochzeiten,*
> *Von Weinen und Klagen,*
> *Von kuehnen Recken Streiten,*
> *Möht Ihr nun Wunderhören sagen."*
>
> DER NIBELUNGEN LIED.

FIRSDT PARDT.

Do oos, in anciend shdory,
Crate voonders ish peen told
Of lapors fool of glories,
Of heroes bluff und bold,
Of high oldt times a-kitin,
Of howlin und of tears,
Of kissin und of vightin :
All dis we likes to hears.

Dere growed once dimes in Schwaben
  Since fifty years pegan,
An shild of decent elders,
  His name Hans Breitemann.
De gross adfentures dat he had,
  If you will only look,
Ish all bescribed so truly
  In dis fore-lying book.

Und allaweil dese lieder
  Vere goin troo his het,
De writer lay von Sonntay,
  A-shleepin in his bett;
Ven lo!—a yellow bigeon
  Coom to him in a dreám,
De same dat Mr. Barnum
  Vonce had in his Muséum.

Und dus out-shpoke de bigeon:
  "If you should brint de songs
Or oder dings of Breitmann
  Vhich to dem on belongs,
Dey will tread de road of Sturm und Drang
  Die wile es möhte leben,
Und pe mis-geborn in pattle
  To dis fate ish it ergeben."

Und dus rebly de dreamer:
"If on de ice it shlip,
Den led it dake ids shanses;
Rip Sam, und let 'er rip!
Dou say'st id vill be sturmy.—
Vot sturmy ish, ish crand.
Crate heroes ish de beoples
In Uncle Samuel's land.

Du bist ein rechter Gelbschnabel
O golden bigeon mine:
Und I'll fighdt id on dis summer
If id dakes me all de line.
Full liddle ish de discount
Oopon de Yankee peeps."
"Go to hell!" exglaim de bigeon:—
Foreby vas all mine shleeps.

SECONDT PARDT.

DERE vent to Sout Carolina,
A shentleman who dinked,
Dat de pallads of der Breitmann
Should papered pe und inked.
Und dat he vouldt fixed de brintin
Pefore de writer know:
Dis make to many a brinter
Fool many a bitter woe.

All in de down of Charleston
A druckerei he found,
Vhere dey cut de copy into takes,
Und sorted it around.
Und all vas goot peginnen,
For no man heeded mooch
Dat half de jours vas Mericans,
Und half of dem vas Dutch.

Und vorser shtill, anoder half
Had vorn de Federal plue,
Vhile de anti-half in Davis grey
Had peen Confeterates true.
Great Himmel!—Vot a shindy
Vos shtarted in de crowd
Vhen some von read Hans Breitmann
His Barty all aloud!

Und von goot-nadured Yankee
  He schvear it vos a shame,
To dell soosh lies on Dutchmen,
  Und make of dem a game.
But dis make mad Fritz Luder,
  Und he schvear dis treat of Hans,
Vos shoost so goot a barty
  Ash any oder man's.

Und dat nodings vos so looscious,
  In all dis eartly shpear,
Ash a quart mug fool of sauer-kraut,
  Mit a plate of lager bier.
Dat de Yankee might pe tam mit himself
  For he, der Fritz, hafe peen
In many soosh a barty,
  Und all dose dings hafe seen.

All mad oopsproong de Yankee,
  Mid all his passion ripe,
Und vired at Fritz mit de shootin-shtick,
  Wheremit he vas settin type.
It hit him on de occiput,
  Und laid him on de floor;
For many a long day afder
  I ween his het vas sore.

Dis roused Piet Weiser der Pfaelzer,
  Who vas quick to act und dink;
He held in hand a roller
  Vhere-mit he vas rollin ink.
Und he dake his broof py shtrikin
  Der Merican top of his het,
Und make soosh a vine impression
  Dat he left de veller for deat.

Allaweil dese dings oonfolded,
  Dere vas rows of anoder kind,
Und drople in de wigwam
  Enough to trife dem plind;
Und a crate six-vooted Soutern man,
  Vot hafe vorked on a Refiew,
Shvear he hope to Gott he mighd pie de forms
  If de Breitmann's book warn't true.

For de Sout vas ploondered derriple,
  Und in dat darksome hour
He hafe lossed a yallow-pine maiden,
  Of all de land de vlower.
Bright gold doblones a hoondered
  He willingly vouldt pay,
Ash soon ash a thrip for a ginger-cake,
  Und deem it sheap dat day.

To him aut-worded a Yorker,
  Who shoomp den dimes de *boun-ti-ee*,
(De only dings *he* lossed in de war
  Was a sense of broperty:)
Says he, "Votefer *you* hafe dropped,
  Some oder shap hafe get,
Und de yallow-pine like him petter ash you;
  On dat it is safe to bet!"

Dead-pale pecame dat Soudern brave,
  He tidn't so moosh as yell;
Boot he drop right onto de Yorker,
  Und mit von lick bust his shell.
Den out he flashed his pig-sticker,
  Und mit looks of drementous gloom,
Rooshed vildly into de pattle
  Dat vas ragin round de room.

Boot, *in angulo*, in de corner,
  Anoder quarrel vas grow
Twix a Boston shap mit a Londoner,
  Und de row ish gekommen so:
De Yankee say dat de H-*u*-mor
  Of Breitmann vas less dan small;
Dough he maket de beoples laughen,
  Boot dat vas only all.

Den a Deutscher say by Donner!
  Dat soosh a baradox
Vould leafe no hope for writers
  In all Pandora's bænder box.
'Twas like de sayin dat Heine
  Hafe no witz in him goot or bad;
Boot he only *kept sayin* witty dings,
  To make beoples pelieve he had.

Den de oder veller be-headed
  Dat dere vas not a shbark of foon
In de Breitmann lieds, vhen you lead dem
  Into English correctly done:
Den a *Proof Sheet* veller res-pondered,
  For he dink de dings vas hard;
"Dat ish shoost like de goot oldt lady
  Ash vent to hear Artemas Ward.

"Und say it vas shames de beoples
  Vas laugh demselfs most tead
At de boor young veller lecturin,
  Vhen he tidn't know vot he said."
Hereauf de Yankee answered:
  "Gaul dern it!—Shtop your fuss!"
Und all de crowd togeder
  Go slap in a grand plug-muss.

De Yankee shlog de Proof Sheet
  Soosch an awfool smack on de face,
Dat he shvell rite oop like a poonkin
  Mit a sense of his tisgrace.
Boot a Deutscher boosted an ink-keg
  On dop of de oders hair,
It vly troo de air like a boomshell—denn—
  Mine Gotts!—Vot a sighdt vas dere!

Denn ofer all de shapel
  Vierce war vas ragin loose;
Fool many a vighten brinter
  Got well ge-cooked his goose;
Fool many an nose mit fisten
  I ween vas padly scrouged;
Fool many an eye pright-gleamin
  Vas ploody out-gegouged.

Dô wart ûfgehauwen
  Dere vas hewin off of pones.
Dô hôrte man dar inne
  Man heardt soosh treadful croans.
Jach waren dâ die Geste
  De row vas rough und tough.
Genuoge sluogen wunden—
  Dere vas plooty wounds enough.

De shpirids of anciend brinters
  From Himmel look down oopon,
Und allowed dat in a *chapel*
  Dere vas nefer soosh carryins-on.
Dere vas Lorenz Coster mit Guttemberg,
  Und Scheffer mit der Fust,
Und Sweynheim mit Pannartz trop deers
  Oopon dis teufel's dust.

Dere vas Yankee jours extincted
  Who lay oopon de vloor;
Dere vas Soutern rebs destructed
  Who nefer vouldt Jeff no more.
Ash deir souls rise oop to Heafen,
  Dey heard de oldt brinters calls;
Und Guttemberg gifed dem all a kick
  Ash he histed dem ofer de walls.

Dat ish de vay dese Ballads
  Foorst vere crooshed in plood und shdorm.
Fool many a day moost bass afay
  Pefore dey dook dis form.
De copy flootered o'er de preasts
  Of heroes lyin todt.
Dis vas de dire peginnin—
  Das war des Breitmann's Noth.

Dis song in Philadelphia
  Long dimes ago pegun;
In Paris vas gondinued, und
  In Dresden ist full-done.
If any toubt apout de *facts*
  In nople minds ish grew,
Let dem ashk Carl Benson Bristed—
  He knows id all ish drue.

Und now dese Breitmann shdories
  Ish geprindt in many a land,
Sogar in far Australia
  Dey're gestohlen und bekannt.
Geh hin mein Puch in alle VVelt,
  Steh auss was dir kompt zu.
Man beysse Dich, man reysse Dich,
  Nur dass man mir nichts thu.

Dranslation.

Go forth my book through all the world,
  Bear what thy fate may be!
They may bite thee, they may tear thee,
  So they do no harm to me!

I Gili Romaneskro.

A Gipsy Ballad.

When der Herr Breitmann vas a yungling, he vas go, bummin aroundt, goot deal in de Worlt, vestigatin human natur, *roulant de vergne en vergne*, ash de Fraentsch boet says: "goin from town to town,"—seein beobles in gemixed sociedy, und learnin dose languages vitch ornamendt a drue moskopolite, or von whose het ish bemost mit experience. Mong oder tongues ash it would appeared, he shpoke fluendly Red Welsh, Black Dootch, Kauder-Waelsch Gaunersprache und Ghipsy, und dis latter languashe he pring so wide dat he write a pook of pallads in it—von of vitch pallads I have intuce him mit moush droples to telifer ofer to de worldt. De inclined reader, vill, mit crate heavy-hood blace pefore himself de fexation und lapor I hafe hat in der Breitmann his absents to get dese Shipsy verses broperly gorrected; as de only shentleman in town who vas culpable of so doin, ish peen gonfined in de town-brison; pout some drobles he hat for shdealin some hens, und pefore I couldt consoolt mit him, he vas rooned afay. Den I fond an oldt vomans Shipsy who vas do nodins boot peg, und so wider mit pout five or four oders more. Derfore der erordoms moast pe excused py de enlightened pooplic who are fomiliar mit dis peautiful languashe, vitch is now so shenerally fashionábel in literary und shpordin circles.

I Gili Romaneskro.

Schunava, ke baschko dela godla
  Schunava Paschomàskro.
Te del miro Dewel tumen
  Dschavena bachtallo.

Schunava apré to ruka
  Chirikló ke gillela:
Kamovéla but dives,
  Eh'me pale kamaveva.

A po je wa'wer divesseste
  Schunava pro gilaviben,
Mákana me avava,
  Pro marzos, pro kuriben.

So korava kuri bente
  So korava apre dróm;
Me kanáv miri romni,
  So kamela la lákero rom.

Dranslation.

I hear de gock a growin!
  I hear de musikant!
Gott gife dee a happy shourney
  Vhen you go to a distand landt.

I hears oopon de pranches
  A pird mit merry shdrain;
Goot many tays moost fanish
  Ere I coom to dis blace again.

Oopon some oder tay-times
  I'll hear dat song from dee;
Boot now I goes ash soldier,
  To war on de rollin sea.

Unt vot I shdeals in pattle,
  Und vot on de road I shdeal,
I'll pring all to my true lofe
  Who lofes her loafer so well.

Steinli von Slang.

FIRSDT PARDT.

DER Watchman look out from his tower,
Ash de Abendgold glimmer grew dim,
Und saw on de road troo de Ganer
Ten shpearmen coom ridin to him:
Und he schvear: "May I lose my next bitter,
Und denn mit der Teufel go hang,
If id isn't dat pully young Ritter,
De hell-drivin Steinli von Slang."

"De vorldt nefer had any such man,
He vights like a sturm in its wrath;
You may call me a recular Dutchmann,
If he arn't like Goliath of Gath.
He ish pig ash de shiant O'Brady,
More ash sefen feet high on a string,
Boot he can't vin de hearts of my lady,
De lofely Plectruda von Sling."

De lady makes welcome her gast in,
  Ash he shtep to de dop of de shtairs;
She look like an angel got lost in
  A forest of autumn-brown hair.
Und a bower-maiden said as she tarried:
  "I wish I may bust mit a bang!
If id isn't a shame she ain't married
  To der her-re-liche Steinli von Slang!"

He pows to de cround fore de lady,
  Vhile his vace ish ash pale ash de tead;
Und she vhispers oonto him a rédè,
  Ash mit arrow point accents she said:
"You hafe long dimes peen dryin to win me,
  You hafe vight, und mine braises you sing;
Boot I'm 'fraid dat de notion ain't in me."—
  De lady Plectruda von Sling.

"Boot brafe-hood teserfes a reward, Sir:
  Dough you've hardly a chost of a shanse.
Sankt Werolf!—medinks id ish hardt, Sir,
  I should allaweil lead you dis dance."
Like a bees ven it booz troo de clofer,
  Dese murmurin accents she flang,
Vhile singin, a stingin her lofer—
  Der woe-moody Ritter von Slang.

" Boot if von ding you do, I'll knock under,
Our droples moost enden damit;
Und if you pull troo it,—by donder!
I'll own myself euchred und bit.
I schvear py de holy Sanct Chlody!
Py mine honor—und avery ding!
You may hafe me—soul, puttons und pody,
Mit de whole of Plectruda von Sling.

" Und dis ish de test of your power:—
Vhile ve shtand ourselfs round in a row,
You moost roll from de dop of dis tower
Down shtairs to de valley pelow.
Id ish rough und ash shteep ash my virtue:
(Mit schwanen shweet accents she sang:)
" Tont dry if you dinks it vill hurt you,
Mine goot liddle Ritter von Slang."

An moormoor arosed mong de beoples;
In fain tid she doorn in her shcorn.
Der votchman on dop of de shdeeples
Plowed a sorryfool doon on his horn.
Ash dey look down de dousand-foot treppé,
Dey schveared dey vouldt pass on de ding,
Und not roll down de firstest tam steppé
For a hoondred like Fraeulein von Sling.

SECONDT PARDT.

'Twas Audumn. De dry leafs vere bustlin
  Und visperin deir elfin-wild talk,
Ven shlow, mit his veet in dem rustlin,
  Herr Steinli coomed out for a walk.
Wild dooks vly afar in de gloamin,
  He hear a vaint gry vrom de gang;
Und vished he vere off mit dem roamin—
  De heart-wounded Ritter von Slang.

Und ash he vent musin und shbeakin,
  He see, shoost aheat in his vay,
In sinkular manner a streakin,
  An strange liddle pein, in cray,
Who toorned on him quick mit a holler,
  Und cuttin a dwo-bigeon ving,
Gried: "Say—can you change me a thaler,
  O, guest of de Lady von Sling?"

De knight vas a goot nadured veller,
  (De peggars all knowed him at sight,)
So he forked out each groschen und heller
  Dill he fix de finances aright.
Boot shoost ash de liddle man vent, he
  (Der Ritter) astonished, cried "Dang!"
For id vasn't von thaler boot *twenty*
  He'd bassed on der Ritter von Slang.

Oh reater!—soopose soosh a vlight in
  De vingers of me, or of you,
How we'd toorned on our heels und gon kitin
  Dill no von vas left to pursue!
Goot Lort!—How *we'd* froze to de ready!
  Boot mit him 'dvas a different ding;
For *he* vent on de high, moral steady,
  Dis lofer of Fraeulein von Sling.

Und dough no von vill gife any gredit
  To dis part of mine dale, shdill ids drue,
He drafelled ash if he vould *dead* it
  Dis liddle oldt man to pursue.
Und loudly he after him hollers,
  Till de vales mit de cliffers loud rang,
"You hafe gifed me nine-ten too moosh dollars—
  Hold hard!" cried de Ritter von Slang.

De oldt man ope his eyes like a casement,
  Und laidt a cold hand on his prow,
Denn mutter in ootmosdt amazement:
  "Vot manner of mordal art dou?
I hafe lifed in dis world a yar tausend,
  Und nefer yed met soosh a ding;
Yet you find it hart vork to pe spouse und
  Peloved py de Lady von Sling!

"Und she vant you to roll from de tower
  Down shteps to yon rifulet shpot."
(Here de knight whom amazement o'erbower
  Gried "Himmelspotzpumpenherr Gott!")
Boot de oldt veller saidt: "I'll arrange it.
  Let your droples und sorrows co hang!
Und no dings vill coom to derange it,
  Pet high on it, Ritter von Slang."

"So get oop dis small oonderstandin;
  Dat to-morrow py ten—do you hear?—
You'll pe mit your *trunk* on de landin;
  I'll pe dere on hand, nefer fear.
Und I dink ve shall make your young voman
  A new kind of meloty sing;
Dat vain, vicked, cruel, unhuman,
  Gott tamnaple Fraeulein von Sling!"

De fiolet shdars vere apofe him,
  Vhite moths und vhite dofes shimmered round,
All nature seemed seekin to lofe him,
  Mit perfume, und vision, und sound.
De liddle oldt feller hat fanished
  In a harp-like melotious twang;
Und mit him all sorrow vas panished
  Afay from der Steinle von Slang.

THIRDT PARDT.

ID vas morn, und de vorldt hat assempled
Mit panners und lances und dust,
Boot de heart of de Paroness trempled,
Und ofden her folly she cussed.
For she found dat der Ritter vould *do it*,
Und "die or get into de Ring,"
Und denn she'd pe cerdain to rue it,
Aldough she vas Lady von Sling.

For no man in Deutschland stood higher
Dan he mit de Minnesing crew;
He vas friendet to Heini von Steier,
Und Wolfram von Eschenbach too.
Und she dinked ash she look from de vinders,
How herzlich his braises dey sang;
"Now dey'll knock my goot name indo flinders
For killin der Ritter von Slang."

Boot oh! der goot knight had a schauer,
Und felt most ongommonly queer,
Ven he find on de dop of de dower
De gray man pesite him appear.
Den he find he no more could go valkin
Und shtood shoost an potrified ding,
Vhile de gray man vent round apout talkin
Und chaffin Plectruda von Sling!

Den at vonce he see indo de problum,
  Und vas stoggered like rats at ids *vim;*
His soul had gone indo de goblum,
  Und de goblum's hat gone into him.
Und de eyes of de volk vas enchanted,
  Dere vas "glamour" oopon de whole gang,
For dey dinked dat dis goblum vitch ranted
  So loose, vas der Ritter von Slang.

Und Lordt! *how* id dalked! Oonder heafens
  Der vas nefer soosh derriple witz,
Knockin all dings to sechses und sefens,
  Und gifin Plectruda Dutch fits.
Mein Gott! how he poonished und chaffed her,
  Like a hell-stingin, devil-born ding,
Vhile de volk lay a-rollin mit laughter
  At Fraeulein Plectruda von Sling.

De lady grew angry und paler,
  De lady grew rat-full und red,
She felt some Satanical jailer
  Hafe brisoned de tongue in her head.
She moost laugh ven she vant to pe cryin,
  Und vas crushed mit de teufelisch clang,
Till she knelt herself, pootty near dyin,
  To dis derriple image of Slang.

Den der goblum shoomp oop to der cieling,
  Und trow sommerseds round on de vloor,
Right ofer Plectruda, a-kneelin,
  Dill she look more a vool dan pefore.
Denn he roll down de shteps light und breezy,
  His laughs made it all apout ring,
Ash he shveared dere vas noding more easy
  Dan to win a Plectruda von Sling.

Und ven he cot down to de pottom,
  He laugh so to freezen your plood;
Und schwear dat de boomps ash he cot em
  Hafe make him veel petter ash good.
Boot—oh—how dey shook at his power,
  Ven he toorned himself roundt mit a bang,
Und roll oop to de dop of de tower
  Vhere he change mit de oder von Slang!

Den all in an insdand vas altered;
  Der Steinli vas coom to himself;
Und de sprite, vitch in double sense paltered,
  From dat moment acain vas an elf.
Dey shdill dinked dat von Slang vas de person
  Who had bobbed oop und down on de ving,
Und knew not who 'tvas lay de curse on
  De peaudiful Lady von Sling.

Nun—endlich—Plectruda—repented,
  Und gazed on der Ritter mit shoy;
In dime to pe married consented,
  Und vas plessed mit a peautiful poy.
A dwenty gold biece on his bosom
  Ven geporn vas tiscofered to hang,
Mit de inscript—" Dis dime don't refuse em."—
  So endet de tale of von Slang.

To a Friend Studying German.

Si liceret te amare,
Ad Suevorum magnum mare
Spousam te perducerem.
[*Tristicia Amorosa. Frau Aventiure, von J. V. Scheffel.*]

VILL'ST dou learn de Deutsche Sprache?
  Den set it on your card
Dat all de nouns have shenders,
  Und de shenders all are hard.
Dere ish also dings called pronoms,
  Vitch ids shoost ash vell to know;
Boot ach!—de verbs or time-words,
  Dey'll work you bitter woe.

Vill'st dou learn de Deutsche Sprache?
  Denn you allatag moost go
To sinfonies, sonatas,
  Or an oratorio.
Ven you dinks you knows 'pout musik,
  More ash any oder man,
Pe sure de soul of Deutschland
  Indo your soul ish ran.

Vill'st dou learn de Deutsche Sprache?
  Dou moost eat apout a peck
A week of stinging sauer-kraut,
  Und sefen pfoundts of shpeck.
Mit Gott knows vot in vinegar
  Und Deuce knows vot in rum:
Dis ish de only cerdain vay
  To make de accents coom.

Vill'st dou learn de Deutsche Sprache?
  Brepare dy soul to shtand
Soosh sendences ash n'er vere heardt
  In any oder landt.
Till dou canst bear parentheses
  Pe twisted ohne Zahl;
Dann wirst du erst Deutschfertig seyn
  For a languashe ideál.

Vill'st dou learn de Deutsche Sprache?
  Du moost, mitout an fear,
Trink efery tay a gallon dry
  Of foamin Sherman bier.
Und de more you trinks, pe cerdain,
  More Deutsch you'll surely pe,
For Gambrinus ish de Emberor
  Of de whole of Germany.

Vill'st dou learn de Deutsche Sprache?
  Pe sholly, brav, und treu,
For dat veller ish kein Deutscher
  Who ish not a sholly poy;
Find out vot means Gemüthlichkeit,
  Und try it mitout fail,
In Sang und Klang dein Lebenlang,
  A heart, ganz krenzfidél.

Vill'st dou learn de Deutsche Sprache?
  If a shendleman dou art,
Denn shdrike right into Deutschland
  Und get a shveetesheart.
From Schwabenland or Sachsen,
  Vhere now dis writer pees,
Und de bretty girls all wachsen
  Shoost like aepples on de drees.

Boot if dou bee'st a lady,
  Denn on de oder hand,
Take a blonde moustachioed lofer,
  In de vine-green Sherman land.
Und if you shouldt kit married,
  Vood mit vood soon makes a vire:
O denn you'll find de Dutch vill coom
  Ash fast as you desire.

Love Song.

O VERE mine lofe a sugar-powl,
  De fery shmallest loomp
Vouldt shveet de seas from bole to bole,
  Und make de shildren shoomp.
Und if she vere a clofer-fieldt
  I'd bet mine only pence
It vould'nt pe no dime at all
  Pefore I'd shoomp de fence.

Her heafenly foice it drill me so,
It really seems to hoort;
She ish de holiest anamile
Dat roons oopon de dirt.
De re'nbow rises ven she sings;
De sonn shine ven she dalk,
De angels crow und flop deir vings
Ven she goes out to valk.

So livin vhite—so carnadine—
Mine lofe's gomblexion glow;
It's shoost like abendcarmosine
Rich gleamin on de shnow.
Her soul makes plooshes in her sheek,
As sommer reds de wein,
Or sonlight sends a fire-life troo
An blank karfunkelstein.

De ueberschwengliche idées
Dis lofe put in my mind,
Vould make a foostrate philosoph
Of any human kind.
'Tis shuderend sweet on eart' to meet
An himmlisch-hoellisch qual,
Und treat mit whiles to kümmel schnapps,
De Shœnheitsideál.

Hans Breitmann As An Uhlan.

With Other New Ballads.

BY CHARLES G. LELAND.

AUTHOR OF "HANS BREITMANN'S PARTY," "HANS BREITMANN ABOUT TOWN," "HANS BREITMANN IN CHURCH," ETC.

Fourth Series of the Breitmann Ballads.

PHILADELPHIA:
T. B. PETERSON & BROTHERS;
306 CHESTNUT STREET.

Contents.

Author's Preface.

THE readers of more than one newspaper will recall that the idea of representing Breitmann as an Uhlan, scouting over France, and frequently laying houses and even cities under heavy contribution, has occurred to very many of "Our Own." A spirited correspondent of the *London Daily Telegraph*, and others of literary fame, have familiarly referred to the Uhlan as Breitmann, indicating that the German-American free-lance has grown into a type; and more than one newspaper, anticipating this volume, has published Anglo-German poems referring to Hans Breitmann and the Prussian-French war. It is, therefore, not remarkable that I should have written the following little book, which I sincerely trust may find as favorable a reception as did its predecessors in the same *genre*.

It is needless, perhaps, to say, that I no more intend to ridicule or satirise the German cause, or the German method of making war, in these poems, than I did those of the American Union, when I first introduced Breitmann as a "bummer" plundering the South. Every army has its unscrupulous stragglers and marauding scouts, whose adventures form good subjects for story and song.

CHARLES G. LELAND.

Extract from a Letter

OF THE SPECIAL CORRESPONDENT

OF THE

"LONDON DAILY TELEGRAPH."

THE Prussian Uhlan of 1870 seems destined to fill in French legendary chronicle the place which, during the invasions of 1814–15, was occupied by the Cossack. He is a great traveller. Nancy, Bar-le-Duc, Commercy, Rheims, Châlons, St. Dizier, Chaumont, have all heard of him. The Uhlan makes himself quite at home, and drops in, entirely in a friendly way, on mayors and corporations, asking not only himself to dinner, but an indefinite number of additional Uhlans, who, he says, may be expected hourly. The Uhlan wears a blue uniform turned up with yellow, and to the end of his lance is affixed a streamer intimately resembling a very dirty white pocket-handkerchief. Sometimes he hunts in couples, sometimes he goes in threes, and sometimes in fives. When he lights upon a village, he holds it to ransom; when he comes upon a city, he captures it, making it literally the prisoner of his bow and his spear. A writer in *Blackwood's Magazine* once drove the people of Lancashire to madness by declaring that, in the Rebellion of 1745, Manchester "was taken by a Scots sergeant and a wench;" but it is a notorious fact that Nancy submitted without a murmur to five Uhlans, and that Bar-leDuc was occupied by two. When the Uhlan arrives in a conquered city, he visits the mayor, and makes his usual inordinate demands for meat, drink, and cigars. If his demands are acceded to, he accepts everything with a grin. If he is refused, he remarks, likewise with a grin, that he will come again to-morrow with three thousand light horsemen, and he gallops away; but in many cases he does not return. The secret of the fellow's success lies mainly in his unblushing impudence, his easy mendacity, and that intimate knowledge of every highway and byway of the country which, thanks to the military organization of the Prussian army, he has acquired in the regimental school. He gives himself out to be the precurser of an imminently advancing army, when, after all, he is only a boldly adventurous free-lance, who has ridden thirty miles across country on the chance of picking up something in the way of information or victuals. Only one more touch is needed to complete the portrait of the Uhlan. His veritable name would seem to be Hans Breitmann, and his vocation that of a "bummer;" and Breitmann, we learn from the preface to Mr. Leland's ballad, had a prototpye in a regiment of Pennsylvania cavalry by the name of Jost, whose proficiency in "bumming," otherwise "looting," in swearing, fighting, and drinking lager beer, raised him to a pitch of glory on the Federal side which excited at once the envy and the admiration of the boldest bushwhackers and the gauntest guerillas in the Confederate host.

Breitmann as an Uhlan.

"Dere vas vonce oopon a dimes a Fräntschman, who asket if a Sherman could have *ésprit*. Allowin for his pad shbellin, de reater vill find dat der Herr Breitmann was have *a spree* goot many dimes. You gant ged round de Dootch.

FRITZ SCHWACKENHAMMER.

HANS BREITMANN'S VISION.

GOTTS blitz! blau Feuer, potz bomben Tod!
Vot shimmers in de mitnacht roth?
Like hell-shtrom boorst o'er heafen's plain,
Trowin dead light on eart acain :—
Ja!—wide im nord om Odin shtone
Lies a shiant form im glare alone,
Troonk py de eis-kalt roarin shdream
Der Hans ish hafe ein wunder tream.
Troonk om haunted Odinstein
Im Hexenlicht und Elfenschein

Vhere blooty Druids omens trew
From grin und screech of shaps dey slew,*
Or vhere der Norseman long of yore
Vas carven eagles on de shore,
As o'er him yell de Valkyr broot
Und crows valk round knee teep im ploot,
Vhile rabens schkreem o'er ruddy bay;
Dere—ten pottles troonk—Hans Breitmann lay.

Fast und rof der war-man shnore
Like de hammer-shlog of Thor,
Schnell ash Mjöllner's bang und beat†
Heaved de form from het to veet,
Vhile apofe him in de shkies
Dere he saw a glorie rise,
Und im mittle von it all
De iron lords of crate Valhall.

Long he gaze mit wölfen glare
At de Aesir‡ in de air.

* "From the palpitations of dying human victims, Druids and Druidesses were wont to draw their auguries."—*The Early Races of Scotland, by Lieut. Col. Forbes Leslie. London*, 1866.

† Mjöllner, The Hammer of Thor.

‡ Gods in the Norse religion.

Long mit shneerin bären grin
He toorn his nase auf und hin
(For ne'er a Sherman—tam de otts—
Vas efer yet gife in to Gotts,)
Dill avery Aes-owned oop dat he
A gott-like man of brass moost pe.

Shtern der Breitmann raise his het,
To his fader Gotts he set:
"Let your worts of wisehood shlip;
Rush your runes, und let 'em rip!
For you de gotts hafe efer pe
Of dose who vere ash gotts to me:—
Alt Thor der Thören here pelow—
Vot hell you vants,* I'd like to know?"

Antworded ash de donner clangs,
Der fader of de iron bangs:
"De gotts will let de hell dogs go,
Und raise damnation here pelow;

* Dese outpressions ish not to pe angeseen py anypodies ash *schvearin,* boot ash inderesdin Norse or Sherman idioms. Goot many refiewers vot refiewsed to admire soosh derms in de earlier editions ish politelich requestet to braise dem in future nodices from a transcendental philological stand-point.

FRITZ SCHWACKENHAMMER.

Until de sassy Frenchmen schmell
De rifers ten dat roon troo hell.
To telle dis I comme dence,
Dou lord of lion impudence.

"Drafeller! I know dee vell!
Breitmann improturbable!
Vhen on eart I hat my shy,
Breitmann of dat age vas I.
I schwear py Thor! so crate und gay,
I smashed de Jötuns in my tay,
Und dow shall pe ge-writ sooplime
Ash de crate *Thor* of deiner time.

"Now ve lets de eagles vly
Skreemin troo de vlamin shky,
Our own specials:—dare nod laugh;
For in de London *Telegraph*,
A voondrous poy vot make oos shdare,
For hop vhat may, he's *alvays dere!*
Vill dell de worlt, troo blut and flame,
Hans Breitmann ist der Uhlan's name.

"Und all dou e'er on eart has done,
From oop gang oontil settin sun,
Vill pe ash nix—I schvear py Thor!
To vat dou'lt do in dieser war;

Plazin roofs und mordered men,
Hell set loose on eart again;
Rush und ride in shtorm und floot,
Cannon roarin, pools of bloot;
Deutschland mad in fool career,
Led py dy Uhlanen speer.
Hell's harfest—sheafs of fictorie,
Reaped mit deat's sword und reapt by dee!

"Ja! On many a dorf und disch,
Dou shalt pring a requisish;*
Dwendy dimes de Fräntscher men
Hafe sporned dy land in blut acain—
All dose dwenty dimes in von,
Py Deutschland shall to France pe done,
Und dwenty dimes in blut and wein
Shalst dou refenge de Palatine.

* *Requisish.* An abbreviation of the word *requisition*, which Breitmann had heard during the War of Emancipation. I once heard this cant term used in a droll manner, about the end of the war, by a little girl, six years old, the daughter of a quartermaster. She had "confiscated," or "foraged," or "skirmished," as it was indifferently called, a toy whip belonging to her little brother of four years, who was clamorously demanding its return. "I cannot let you have the whip," said she gravely, "as I need it for military purposes; but I can give you a requisish for it on my papa, who will give you an order on the United States Government."

C. G. L.

" Go!—mit shpeer und fiery muth!
Go!—mit durst for bier und blut!
Go!—mit lofe for Vaterland,
Into burning fury fanned:
Towns und hen-roosts shall hafe shown
Vhere der Uhlan ist peen gone,
Und cocks vill cut und men crow tame
To hear of der Uhlanen name."

Der fision fadet in de shky,
Und hours vent on und time goed py,
Vot heardest dou Napolium!
De rumpitty, rumpitty, rumpitty poom!
Ven you hear de sound of de droom,
Oh denn you know dat de Dootch hafe coom,
De treadful roarin Dootch mit de droom
Und de roompitty, pumpitty, poompitty pum!
De wild ferocious Dootch on a bum
Mit sworts vot shblit de cranium,
In cannon roar und pattle hum,
Mit fee und faw on de foe und fum!
Led py de awful Breitemum!
    Bitty boom!!
    Boom!

BREITMANN IN A BALLOON.

WHO vas efer hear soosh voonders,
  Holy breest or virshin nonn?
As pefelled de Coptain Breitmann,
  Vhen he hoont an air-ballon.
Der Bizzy* und der Dizzy,†
  Mit Lothairingen und Lothair,
Vas nodings to dis Deutscher,
  Who vent kitin troo de air.

Id was im yar Nofember,
  In eighdeen sefendee,
Der Breitmann vent a prowlin,
  By monden light vent he.
In fillages deserted
  He hear de Uhu moan;
For you alvays hear der Uhu ‡
  Vhere der Uhu-lan ish gone.

* Bismarck. † Disraeli.

‡ *Uhu.* An owl—the bird of kn-*owl*-edge.

Alone *allonsed* * der Uhlan,
  Boot nodings could he find
Safe whitey clouds a drivin
  In moonshine fore de wind.
Boot ash he see dese cloudins
  He bemark dat *von* vas round,
Und inshtead of goin oopwarts
  It kep risin towards de ground.†

"Oh, vot ish dis a gomin?
  Some planet, py de Lord!
Too boor to life in heafen,
  Coom down on eart to poard;
Und pelow it schwing tree engels—
  Two he-vons mit a wench.
Boot, mein Gott! vot sort of engels
  Can dose pe, dalkin Fræntsch!

"I hafe read in Eckhartshausen
  Dat oop in heafen—py tam!
De engels dalk in Sherman,
  Und sing Mardin Luther's psalm.

* *Allons.* Uhlan slang for *go* or *went*, as in America they use the Spanish word *vamos* to express every person in every sense of the verb *to go*. Pronounce *allon'd*.

† "Mine bread rises downwarts dis dime, I dink."
Tales, by J. K. PAULDING.

O nein—es sind kein engeln
  Vot sail so smoofly on,
Das sind verfluchte Franzosen
  In einem luft-ballon!"*

Hei! how der Breitmann streak it
  Ven vonce he kess de trut'!
He spurred id like de wild fire
  Of hope in early yout'.
Troo de weingarts like der teufel
  Vhen he shase a lawyer's soul;
Down der moundain mit his lanze
  Und his wafin banderol.

Down de moundain, o'er de valley,
  Troo de village he ish gone;
Dog-barks die out pehind him,
  Oders bark ash he come on.
Liddle heedet he deir bellin,
  Liddle mind der Hahnen crow;
Liddle hear dur Bauren yellin,
  Clotter, clodder, on he go.

* "O no, those are no angels
  Which sail so smoothly on.
O no—they're curséd Frenchmen
  All in an air-balloon.'

" Oh, vot ish hoontin foxen,
  Und vot ish yäger pliss,
Und vot ish shasin bison
  On de blains, to soosh ash dis ?
I hafe dinked dat roonin rebels
  Vas de pest of eartly fun;
Boot id isn't half so sholly
  Ash to go a luft-ballon."

Und ash id shdill vent onwart,
  Shdill onwarts mit der wind,
Dere coom a real madness
  To catch id o'er his mind.
Und had'st dou seen him vlyin,
  Dat wild onfuriate brick,
Dou'st hafe schworn dat Coptain Breitmann
  Was pecome balloonatic.

In fain dey trow deir sand-bags,
  In fain all dings let fall,
De ballon shdill kep a sinkin,
  Und id vouldn't rise at all.
Yet de wild wind trife id onwarts,
  Onwarts shdill der Breitmann go,
Dill he cotch id py a rope-ent
  Vot vas hangin town pelow.

Boot vhen it risen oopwarts,
  Ash he gling to id, of corse,
Mit der lefter hand he holtet
  To de pridle of his horse.
Der horse valk on his hind-legs :
  Too schwer to rise vas he;
Mein Gott! vot fix for Breitmann
  Of de Uhlan cavallrie!

So he go for seferal stunden
  Petween himmel und eart pelow,
Boot der teufel und die engels
  Couldn't make der Hans let go.
Dill all at vonce an idée
  Coom from his loocky shtar—
He led co his horse's pridle
  Und glimb oop indo de car.

Und vot you dinks he foundet
  Vhen in dat air-ballón?
A nople Englisch vicomte,
  Milord de Robinson;
Und mit him vas a laity
  Mit whom he'd rooned afay,
Whom he introduce to Breitmann
  Ash die Jungfer Salomé.

Und der dritte was a barson,
  Whom Milord, mit prudent view,
Hat took als secretairé,
  Likevise for pallast doo.
Dey should hafe bitched him ofer
  Vhen de gas was out, dey say;
Boot de damé vould not 'low it:—
  She'd an arrière pensée.

Sait Milord: "Afar we've wandered,
  We are done completely brown;
And I'll give a thousand shiners
  If you'll take me to a town
Where no one will molest us
  Till we find our way to Lon—."
Here der Breitmann ent de sentence
  Ash he gry out, shortly, "*done!*"

"And as for this fair lady
  To whom I would be bound,"
Said Milord, "we'll have a wedding
  Before we reach the ground.
To escape her father's anger
  We fled to live in peace,
But she's relatives in London,
  And *they* have—the police."

O vas not dis a voonders
  To make de Captain shdare?—
A tausend pounds in bocket
  Und a veddin in de air?
He gafe avay de laity
  Und als sie wieder kam
Zur festen Erde weider
  Ward sie Robinson Madame.*

"O go mit me," said Breitmann,
  "O go in mein Quartier!
Don't mind denm gommon soldiers,
  For I'm an officier."
He guide dem troo de coontry
  Till dey reach de ocean strand;
Now dey sit und pless Hans Breitmann
  In de far-off English land.

Dis ish Breitmann's last adfenture
  How troo Himmel air flew he:
Und it's dime, oh nople reader!
  For a dime to part from dee.
Dou may'st dake it all in earnest
  Or pelieve id's only fon;
Boot dere's woonder dings has hoppent
  Fery oft in Luft-ballón.

* And when she came adown
Unto the earth's firm surface,
She was Mrs. Robinson.

BREITMANN AND BOUILLI.

"Très estimé ami,—Ick seyn nock nit verdorb,
Vielleickt Sie denck wohl kar, das ick sey tod gestorb,
Ock ne Kott loben Danck, ick leb nock kanss wohl auf.
. . . .
Naturlich wie Kespenst die off die Kasse keh."
—*Deutsch-Franzos, Leipzig*, 1736.

VOT roombles down de Bergstrass?
Vot a grash ish in de air!
Mit a desberate gonfusion,
Und a gry of wild tespair;
Das sind gethräsht Franzosen,*
Und dose who after flee
Are de terror of Champagner,
Die Uhlan cavallrie.

So liddle say die hoonted,
De hoonters lesser shdill;
Der Frank is ride for's leben,
Der Deutscher rides to kill.

* Those are thrashed Frenchmen.

Ofer dickly-doosty faces
  Deir eyes like wild-katz's glare;
De blut und iron ridin
  Of furie und despair.

Boot of all de wild Uhlanen,
  Der Breitmann ride de pest;
For he mark de Fränisch gommanter
  Ish most elegandtly tresst.
Und ash he coom down on him,
  Dere's a deat' look in his eye:
"Gotts! if I carfe dat toorkey,
  How I'll make de stoofin vly!"

Mit a clotter und a flotter,
  Like a hell-sturm dey are on;
Mit a rottle to de pattle
  Coom de Deutschers, knockin' down,
Down de moundain to a brucké—
  Vhy die Fräntschmen toorn ad bay?
Oder Deutsch were dere pefore dem,
  Und die pridge ish coot avay!

Von second der Franzose
  Look down mit blitzen eye;
Von second at de brucké,
  Den toorn him round to die.

Vhile mit out-ge-poke-te lanze,
  Like ter teufel shot from hell,
Rode der ploonder-shtarvin Breitmann
  On der grau-bart Colonél.

Vot for der Captain Breitmann
  Ish shdop in his career?
Vot for he pool his pridle?
  Vot for let down his śpeer?
Vot for his eyes like saucers
  Grow pigger, rimmed mit staub?
Vot for his hair, a pristlin,
  Lift oop his pickel-haub?*

So awfool—so oneart'ly,
  So treadful was his glare,
So unbeschreiblich gastly,
  Dat der Colonel self was shkare.
Oop come der Breitmann ridin,
  Und mit gratin foice he said:
"Bist—du—wirkelich—lebendig?†
  Can de grafe gife oop its tead?

* Der Uhlan vas nod shenerally wear pickel-häube, but dis tay der Herr Breitmann gebappant to hafe von on.

FRITZ SCHWACKENHAMMER.

† "And art thou truly living?"

"Dou livest yet—dou breaf 'st yet,
Dough oldter now you pe
Since I mordered you in Strasburg,
Mein freund—mon Jean Bouilli.
We lofed de selfe maiden
Wohl forty years agone:—
She died to hear I kilt you:—
Jean—how weiss your beard ish grown!

"I would gife my Hab' und Güter,*
Dereto mein bit of life,
Couldt I pring dat shild to leben,
Und make her, Jean, dy wife!"
Here der Breitmann boorst out gryin,
Like a liddle prook vept he;
Und dey hugged and gissed einander,
Der Breitmann und Bouilli.

"Ach, de efils dat from efil
Troo a life ish efer grow!
Had I nefer dink I killed you,
Many a man were livin now—
Many a man dat shleeps in canebrakes,
Many a man py pillow-shore;
For dy morder mate me reckelos,
Und *von* tead man gries for more!

* "All my property."

"O, Mädchen! schön im Himmel! *
  (Warst schön on eart' difine)—
Can'st dink among de Engeln
  Of soosh as me und mine?
Den look on soosh a Reue,
  Ash eart' has nefer known:—
Whereto hast dou a sabre?
  Wherefore not kill me, Jean?"

"O, ne pleurez pas, mon Breitmann!
  Je trouve cela trop fort,"
Gry der Colonel sehr politelich;
  "*How!*—you crois dat I was *mort!*
Mon Dieu! 'Tis but one minute,
  As we galloped to this plain,
I thought your spear, mon gaillard,
  Would kill me o'er again.

"Je vous fais mon compliment,
  Your tendreese becomes you well;
Et ne pleurez pas, mon brave,
  Pour la petite demoiselle.
I have had a thousand since;
  One can always find such game;
Et pour dire la vérité,
  I have quite forgot her name."

* "O maiden fair in Heaven!"

Der Breitmann look so earnest,
  Long and earnest at his foe,
Ash if seein troo his augen
  To de forty years ago.
Mit *vot* a shmile der Breitmann
  Toorned roundt und rode away:
Dat was all his parting greetin
  To der Cólonél Français.

BREITMANN TAKES THE TOWN OF NANCY.

O HEAR a wondrous shdory
  Vot soundet like romance,
How Breitmann mit four Uhlans
Vas dake de town of Nantz.
De Fräntschmen call it Nancy.*
Und dey say its very hard
Dat Nancy mit her soldiers
Vas getook py gorpral's guard.

* Nancy, the "light of love" of Lorraine.—*London Times*, Dec. 6, 1870.

Dey dink id vas King Wilhelm
Ash Hans ride in de down,
Und like Odin in his glorie
Gazed derriply aroun'.
Denn mit awfool condesenchen
He at de Fräntschmen shtare,
Und say, "Ye wretsched shildren!
Abbortez mir vodre mère!"

Hans mean de city Syndic,
Vhom *maire* de Frântschmen call;
So mit a tousand soldiers
Dey 'scort him to de Hall:
In de shair of shtade dey sot him,
Der maire coom to pe heard,
Und Hans glare at him fife minutes
Pefore he shbeak a word.

Den in iron dones he ootered:
"Ich temand que rentez fous:
Shai dreisig mille soldaten
Bas loin l'ici, barploo!
Aber tonnez-moi Champagner;
Shai an soif exdrortinaire—

Apout one douzaine cart-loads;
Und dann je fous laisse faire."*

Denn he say to Schwackenhammer,
His segretairé—" Read
A liddle exdra listé
Of dings de army need,
Und dell dem in Französisch
Dey moost shell de neetfool down
In less dan dwendy minudes,
Or, py Gott, I'll purn de town."

" *Item*—on tousand vatches
Of purest gold so fair;
Dazu fünf tousand silbern,
For de gommon soldiers' wear;
Und tree dousand diamant ringé
Dey moost make tirectly come,
We need dem for our schweethearts
Ven we write to em at home!

* "I require you to surrender:
I have thirty thousand men
Not far from here, parbleu!
But give me first champagne;
I've a wondrous thirst, you know—
About a dozen cart-loads;
And then I'll let you go."

" Von million cigarren
Ve'll accept ash extra boons
For not squeezin dem seferely,
Dazu dwelf tousend shboons."
Here der maire fell down in schwoonin,
Denn all dat he could say
Vas " O mon dieu de dieu, dieu!
Nous voilà ruinées!"*

No wort der Breitmann ootered,
He only make a sgratch,
Calm and silend, on de daple,
Mit a liddle friction match.
De maire versteh de motion,
So went him to de task
Of raisin mong de peoples
Vot it vas der Breitmann ask.

So kam he mit de ringé
Dey vind dem pooty soon;
So kam he mit de vatches,
Und avery silber spoon.
Boot ash for de champagner
He wept and loudly call
Dat *par dieu!* he hadn't any,
For de Deutsch hafe troonk it all.

* " O Lord, Lord, Lord!
We are ruined!"

Ja!—de gorporal's guart have trinket
Efery pottle in de down,
Vhile dese negotiations
Oop-stairs vere written down.
Boot der Breitmann sooplimely,
Like von who nodings felt,
Said, "Instet of le champagner
Nous brentirons du gelt.*

"Ja wohl! Donnes cent mille franken,
C'est mir égal, you know;†
Pid dem pring id in a horry,
For 'tis dime for oos to go."
Der maire he pring de money,
Und der Breitmann squeeze his hand,—
"Leb wohl, dou nople brickbat,
Herzbruder in Frankenland!

"Boot it griefes my soul to larmen,
Und I sypatize mit dein,
To *pense* of you, mon ami,
Sans le champagner wein.
Dere will oder Deutsch pe gomin,
Und it preak mine heart to dink

* "We will take the ready *gelt.*"

† "Yes, give a hundred thousand francs,
'Tis all one to me, you know."

De vay dey'll bang and slang you
If dere's no champagne to trink!

"Cela fous fera miseré
Que she ne feux bas see;
So, vollow mes gonseillés,
Et brenez mon afis.
Shai, moi, deux mille boutelles,
De meilleur dat man can ashk,*
Vich I will gladly sell—
Sheap as dirt—ten franks a flask."

De maire look oop to heafen,
Wohl nodings could he say.
Vhile oud indo de mitnight
Der Breitmann rode afay.
Away—atown de falley,
Till noding more abbears
Boot de glitter of de moonlight,
De moonlight on deir spears.

* "Ah, that will make you trouble,
Which I would not gladly see;
So, follow all my counsels,
And take advice from me
I have, two thousand bottles,
The best——"

Breitmann in Bivouac.

HE sits in bivouacke,
  By fire, peneat' de drees;
A pottle of champagner
  Held shently on his knees;
His lange Uhlan lanze
  Stuck py him in de sand;
Vhile a goot peas-poodin' sausage
  Adorn his oder hand.

Und jungere Uhlanen
  Sit round wit oben mout'
To hear der Breitmann's shdories
  Of fitin in de Sout.'
Und he gife dem moral lessons,
  How pefore de battle pops:
"Take a liddle brayer to Himmel,
  Und a goot long trink of schnapps."

Den his leutenant bemarket:
  "How voonder shdrange it peen
Dat so very many wild pigs
  Ish dis year in de Ardennes.
Ash I scout dere—donner'r 'wetter!—
  I sah dem coom heraus,
Shoost here und dere an Eber
  Mit a hoondert tousand saus.

"Shost dink of all dese she-picks
  Vor flet to neutral land!"
Said Breitmann: "Fery easy
  Ish dis to oonderstand:
Dese schwein-picks mit de sauen
  Vot you saw a-roonin rond,
Ish a crate medempsygosis
  Of the Fräntsché demi-monde.

"I hafe readet in de Bible
  How soosh a coterie
Vas ge-toornet indo swine-picks,
  Und roon down indo de see;
Boot since de see aint handy,
  Or de picks vere all too dumm,
Dey hafe coot agross de porder
  Und vly to Belgium."

Now ash dey boorst oud laughin,
  Und got more liquor out,
Dey hearden from de sendry
  A shot and denn a shout.
Und Breitmann crasp his sabre
  Quich ash de bullet hiss,
Und leapin out, demantet,
  "Her'r'r'r Gott! vat row ish dish?"

Und bold der Schwabian answert:
  "Dis minute on de ground
Dere coomed a Fräntschman greepin,
  On all-fours a-prowlin round.
I ask him vat he vanted;
  Werda! I gry; boot he
Say nodings to my shallenge,
  Und only answer '*Oui.*'

"So I shoot him like der teufels,
  Und I rader dink our friend,
Dis sneakin Frank-tiroir,
  Ish a-drawin to his end."
So dey hoonted in de pushes,
  Und in avery gorner dig,
Boot, mein Gott! how dey vas laughen,
  Ven dey found a—mordered pig.

Next week dey hear from Paris,
  Und reat in de *Gaulois*
Of de most adrocious action
  Der vorlt vas efer saw.
How de Uhlan cannibalen,
  Dis vile und awful prood,
Hafe killt a nople Fräntschman,
  Und cut him oop for food.

"Ja—shop him indo sausage,
  Und coot him indo ham;
Und schwear dey'll serfe all oders
  Exacdly so—py tam!
Sons of France, awake to glory,
  Let your anciend valor shine!
Und schweep dis Prussian vermin
  Het und dails indo de Rhine!

BREITMANN'S LAST PARTY.

For fear of some missed onder standings, I vould shtate, dat dis is only mean de last Barty dat der Herr Coptain Breitmann has ge given—*as yed.* Pimepy I kess he gife anoder von, und if I kits an in-leading, or indrotuckshun, I kess I'll go. I am von of de vellers dat vos ad de virst Barty, vhere mine cousine de Madilda Yane vas tantz mit Herr Breitmann.

FRITZ SCHWACKENHAMMER,
Olim Studiosus Theologiæ, now Uhlan free-lancer,
and Segretarius of Coptain Breitmann

VOT gollops at midnight,
  Mit *h'roolah* and yell,
Like der teufel's wild yäger
  Boorst loose out of hell?
Vot cleams in the sunrise
  Bright vlashin in gold?
Das sind die Uhlanzers
  Of Breitmann der bold.

Dey frighten de coontry,
  Dey ploonder de toun;
And when dey are oop
  Die Franzosen co doun;
For pefore de wild Norsemen
  De Southron must flee:
Ab ira Normannorum
  Libera nos Domine!*

How dey sweep de chateux!
  How dey grab oop de hens!
Und gobble de toorkeys
  Shoot oop in de pens!
Like de Angel of Deat'
  Dey are ragin abroad:
You may track dem py fedders
  Knee-deep in de road.

O der Breitmann ish on,
  Und der Breitmann is on,
Und mit him de Uhlans
  Are ploonderin gone.
De demon of fengeance
  His wings o'er em vave,
Mit deir fingers like hooks,
  Und de breat' of de grafe.

* From the wrath of the Northmen, deliver us, Lord!

Dey coom to a castel,
  So shplendid, of bricks
Franzosen defend it.
  Das help em gar nichts.
For de Uhlans hafe take it,
  Dey smash in de gate,
Und inshpired by Gott's fury,
  Dey shdole all de plate.

From shamber to shamber
  Dey fighted deir way,
Till dead in de hall
  De Franzosen all lay;
Und dere shtood a mädchen
  So lieblich und hold,
Who laugh at de dead
  Troo her ringlocks of gold.

Den der Breitmann, all plooty,
  To'm mädel so lind,
Spoke courtly und tender:
  "Vy laughst dou, mein kind?"
Denn de plue-eyed young peaudy,
  Mit lippe so red,
Said, "Vy *not* shall I laughen?
  Dose Frenchmen are dead.

" I coom hear from Deutschland,
  De shildren to teach ;
Dey mock me for Deutsch,
  Und dey sneer at mine sbeech ;
Und since de war komm,
  Dey vas nearly gone mad,
You wouldn't peliefe
  How dey dreet me so pad."

Mit a tear Breitmann bend,
  To de peaudifool miss ;
" Crate Gott ! cans't dou suffer
  Soosh horrors ash dis ?"
His arm round de maiden
  Der hero has bound,
Und it shtaid dere goot vhile,
  'Fore dey got it unwound.

" Ho ! fetch me de diamonds !
  Ho ! shell out de rings !
Mit all in de castle
  Of dat sort of dings."
'Twas brought to de Captain—
  A donderin load :
At de veet of de mädchen
  Dat ploonder he trowed.

"Ho! pring oos champagner!
  Und light oop de hall!
Dis night der Herr Breitmann
  Will gife you a ball.
Dat pile of dead vellers,
  Vot died for La France,
May see, if dey like,
  How de Shermans can tance."

Dey find laties' garments,
  Und—troot to confess—
Likewise som Fräntsch maidens,
  Who help dem to tress.
De rest of de Uhlans,
  Who hadn't soosh loves,
Fixed oop in black clothes
  Mit white chokers und gloves.

Now hei! for de fittles!
  Und hei! for clavier!
For de tantz of de Uhlans—
  De men of de speer!
How de shendlemen ashk
  If dey'd blease introduce;
How de ladies mit beards
  Were called Espionnes Prusses!

Hei, ho! how dey tanzét!
  Hei, ho! how dey sang!
How mit klingen of glasses
  De braun arches rang!
How dey trill from deir hearts,
  Ash dey pour out der wein,
De songs of de Oberland,—
  Songs of der Rhein!

Und madder und wilder,
  All whirlin around,
Vent Hans mit de maiden
  In Bacchanal bound.
She helt to his peard,
  Und dey gissed as if mad;
I tont dink dat efer
  Vas dimes like dey had.

Boot calm in de hall,
  Ever calm on de floor,
Was a row of still guests
  Dat wouldt tantz nefermore.
Mit plood shtreams black winding,
  Der lord mit his men,
When der Youngest Day cooms
  Hans may meet dem acain.

Hoorah for der Uhlan,
  So rash und so wild!
Hoorah for der Uhlan,
  Der teufel's own child!—
Dis ish "Breitmann's Last Barty,"
  Dey'll sing it for years;
De lords of de lanzes,
  De sons of de speers.

For dey frighten de coontry,
  Dey ploonder de toun;
Und when dey are oop
  De Franzosen go doun;
For pefore de wild Norsemen
  Weak Southrons moost flee:
Ab ira Normannorum
  Libera nos Domine!

Hans Breitmann In Europe.

With Other New Ballads.

BY CHARLES G. LELAND.

AUTHOR OF "HANS BREITMANN'S PARTY," "HANS BREITMANN ABOUT TOWN," "HANS BREITMANN IN CHURCH," "HANS BREITMANN AS AN UHLAN," "MEISTER KARL'S SKETCH-BOOK."

Fifth Series of the Breitmann Ballads.

PHILADELPHIA:
T. B. PETERSON & BROTHERS;
306 CHESTNUT STREET.

Contents.

Hans Breitmann in Europe.

BREITMANN IN PARIS.

(1869.)

"Recessit in Franciam."

"Et affectu pectoris,
Et toto gestu corporis,
Et scholares maxime,
Qui festa colunt optime."
—*Carmina Burana*, 13*th century*.

DER teufel's los in Bal Mabille,
Dere's hell-fire in de air,
De fiddlers can't blay noding else
Boot Orphée aux Enfers;
Vot makes de beoples howl mit shoy?
Da capo—bravo!—bis!!
It's a Deutscher aus Amerikà:
Hans Breitmann in Paris.

14

Dere's silber toughts vot might hafe peen,
  Dere's golden deed vot *must:*
Der Hans ish come to Frankenland
  On one eternal bust.
Der same old rowdy Argonaut
  Vot hoont de same oldt vleece,
A hafin all de foon dere ish—
  Der Breitmann in Paris.

Mit a gal on eider shoulder
  A holdin py his beard,
He tantz de Cancan, sacrament:
  Dill all das Volk vas skeered.
Like roarin hippopotamos,
  Mit a kangarunic shoomp,
Dey feared he'd smash de Catacombs,
  Each dime der Breitmann bump.

De pretty liddle cocodettes
  Lofe efery dings ish new,
"D'ou vient il donc ce grand M'sieu?
  O sacré nom de Dieu!"
In fain dey kicks deir veet on high,
  And sky like vlyin geese,
Dey can not kick de hat afay
  From Breitmann in Paris.

O vhere vas id der Breitmann life?
  Oopon de Rond Point gay,
Vot shdreet lie shoost pehind his house?
  La rue de Rabelais.
Aroundt de corner Harper's shtands
  Vhere Yankee drinks dey mill,
Vhile shdraight ahet, agross de shdreet,
  Der lies de Bal Mabille.

Id's all along de Elsées,
  Id's oop de Boulevarce,
He's sampled all de weinshops,
  Und he's vinked at efery garçe.
Dou shveet plack-silken Gabrielle,
  O let me learn from dee,
If 'tis in lofe—or absinthe drunks,
  Dat dis wild ghost may pe?

Und dou may'st kneel in Notre Dame,
  Und veep away dy sin,
Vhile I go vight at Barriere balls,
  Oontil mine poots cave in;
Boot if ve pray, or if ve sin—
  Vhile nodings ish refuse,
'Tis all de same in Paris here,
  So long ash *l' on s' amuse.*

O life, mein dear, at pest or vorst,
  Ish boot a vancy ball,
Its cratest shoy a vild *gallop*,
  Vhere madness goferns all.
Und should dey toorn ids gas-light off,
  Und nefer leafe a shbark,
Sdill I'd find my vay to Heafen—or—
  Dy lips, lofe, in de dark.

O crown your het mit roses, lofe!
  O keep a liddle sprung!
Oonendless wisdom ish but dis:
  To go it vhile you're yung!
Und Age vas nefer coom to him,
  To him Spring plooms afresh,
Who finds a livin' spirit in
  Der Teufel und der Flesh.

BREITMANN IN LA SORBONNE.

DER Breitmann sits in La Sorbonne,
  A note-pook in his hand,
'Tvas dere he vent to lectures,
  Und in oldt Louis le Grand.

Id's more ash two und dwendy years
  Since here I used mein pen;
Oh, where ish all de characders,
  Dat I hafe known since denn?

Der cratest boet efer vas,
  Der pest I efer known,
Vent lecdures here, too, shoost like me,
  Le Sieur Françoys Villon.
He raise de teufel all arount,
  He hear de Sorbonne chime;
Crate shpirid ender in mein heart,
  Und mofe mein soul to rhyme.

Balade.

Dictes moy—in what shpirit land
  Ish Clara Lafontaine?
Or Pomaré, or La Frisette,
  Who blazed on soosh a train?
Shveet Echo flings de quesdion pack,
  O'er lake or shdreamlet lone;
All eartly peauty fades afay,
  Vhere ish dem lofed ones gone?

Oh, vhere ish Lola Montez now,
  So lofed in efery land?
How oft I shmoked dose cigarettes
  She rollt mit vairy hand!
Dat mighdy soul, dat shplendit brick,
  A saint's pecrme to be,
For mit soosh saints der Breitmann make
  His Hagiologie.

Und vhere ish La Pochardinette?
  Ish she too mit de dead?
She lofed de Latin Quarter mit
  A hat und fedder on her het.
Lebe wohl petite Pochardinette!
  Qui ne safait refuser,
Ni la ponche à la bleine ferre,
  Ni sa pouche à un paiser.

O Prince! dese quesdions all are nix,
  I sit here all alone,
Mit von refrain to end de shdrain,
  Vhere ish mein lofed vons gone?
Vhen Marcovitch has cut und run,
  Und Schneider's off de ving,
Some cray old reprobate like me
  Vill of dese lofed vons sing.

BREITMANN IN FORTY-EIGHT.

DERE woned once a studente,
  All in der Stadt Paris,*
Whom jeder der ihn kennte,
  Der rowdy Breitmann hiess.
He roosted in de rue La Harpe,
  Im Luxembourg Hotel,
'Twas shoost in anno '48,
  Dat all dese dings pefel.

Boot he who vouldt go hoontin now
  To find dat rue La Harpe,
Moost hafe oongommon shpecdagles,
  Und look darnation sharp.
For der Kaisar und his Hausmann
  Mit hauses made so vree,
Dere roon shoost now a Bouleverse
  Vhere dis shdreet used to pe.

* There is a German student's song which begins with this couplet.

In dis Hotel de Luxembourg,
  A vild oldt shdory say,
A shtudent vonce pring home a dame,
  Und on de nexter day,
He pooled a ribbon from her neck—
  Off fell de lady's het;
She'd trafelled from de guillotine,
  Und valked de city—deadt.

Boot Breitmann nefer cared himself
  If dis vas falsch or drue,
I kess he hat mit lifin gals
  Pout quite enough to do.
Und Februar vas gomin,
  Ganz revolutionnaire,
Und vhere der Teufel had vork on hand,
  Der Hans vas alvays dere.

Und darker grew de beople's brows,
  No Banquet could dey raise,
So dey shtood und shvore at gorners,
  Or dey singed de Marseillaise.
Und here und dere a crashin sound
  Like forcin shutters ran,
Und boorstin gun-schmidt's vindows in
  Hard vorked der Breitemann.

He helped to howl Les Girondins,
  To cheer be beople's hearts;
Me maket dem bild parricades
  Mit garriages und garts.
Vhen a bretty maiden sendinel
  Vonce ask der countersign,
He gafe das kind a rousin giss,
  Gott hute dir und dein!

Und wilder vent de pattle,
  France spread her oriflamme,
Und deeper roared de sturm-bell,
  De bell of Notre Dame;
Und he who nefer heard it,
  O'er shots und cries of fear,
Loud booming like a dragon's roar,
  Has someding yet to hear.

Und in de Faubourg Sainte Antoine
  Dere comed a fusillade,
Und dyin groans und fallin deadt
  Vere roundt dat parricade.
But der song of Revolution
  From a tousand voices round,
Made a fearful opera gorus
  To de deat' gries on de ground.

Und all around dose parricades
  Dey raise der teufel dere;
Somedimes dey vork mit pig-axes,
  Und somedimes mit gewehr.
Dey maket prifate houses
  Gife all deir arms afay,
Und denn oopon de panels
  Dey writet *Armes données.*

Und ve saw mid roarin vollies,
  Shtreaked like banded settin suns,
Two regiments coome ofer,
  Und telifer oop deir guns.
Hei!—how de deers vere roonin:
  Hei!—how dey gryed hurrahs!
For dey saw de vight vas ofer,
  Und dey know dey gained deir cause.

Dus spoke deir hearts outboorstin,
  In battle by de blade,
From sun tó sun mit roarin gun
  Und donnerin parricade.
In vain pefore de depudies
  De princes tremblin stood,
Vot cooms in France too late a day
  Cooms shoost in dime for blood.

Vhen de Tuileries vas daken,
  Amid de scotterin shot,
Und vlyin stones, und howlin,
  Und curses vild und hot.
'Tvas dere Hans clobbed his musket,
  Und dere de man vas first
To roosh into de palace,
  Ven de toors vere in-geburst.

Some vellers burn de guart-haus,
  Some trink des Königs wein;
Some fill deir hats mit rasbry sham,
  Un prandy beeches fein.
Hans Breitmann in de gitchen
  Vas shdare like avery ding,
To see vot lots of victual-de-dees
  Id dakes to feed a king.

Und oder volk, like plackguarts,
  Vent dook de goaches out;
Und burnin dem, dey rolled dem
  Afay mit yell und shout.
Der Brietmann in der barlor,
  Help writen rapidly,
La liberté pour la Pologne!
  Likevise—*pour l'Italie!*

Den in der Tuileries courtyard
  Ten tousand volk come on;
Dey vas gissin und hurrahin
  For to dink der king vas gone.
Some vas hollerin und tantzin
  Round de blazin oldt caboose
Vhen Fräntschmen kits a goin,
  Den dey lets der teufel loose.

Boot von veller set me laughin,
  Who roosh madly roun de field;
He hat rop de Cluny Museum,
  Und gestohlen speer und schild.
Mit a sblentit royal charger,
  Vitch he hat somevhere found,
Like a trunken wild Don Quixote,
  He vent tearin oop und round.

Doun vent de line of Bourbons,
  Doun vent de vork of years,
Ash de pillars of deir temple
  Ge-crashed like splintered speers;
Und o'er dem rosed a phantom,
  Wild, beautiful, und weak,
Vhile millions gry arount her—
  Vive! vive la Republique!

Tree days mid shdiflin powder shmoke,
  Tree days mid cheers und groans,
Ve fought to guard de parricades,
  Or pile dem oop mit shtones.
De hand vitch held de bistol denn,
  Or made de crowbar bite,
Das war de same Hans Breitmann's hand
  Vitch now dese verses write.

Breitmann in Belgium.

Vlaenderen, dag en nacht
  Denk ik aen u.
Waer ik ook ben en vaer,
Gy zyt my altyd naer.
Vlaenderen, dag en nacht
  Denk ik aen u.

Overal vrolykheid,
  Overal lust.
Maegden van fier gelaet,
Knapen zoo vroom en draet,
Overal vrolykheid,
  Overal lust.

Hoffmann von Fallersleben.

BREITMANN IN SPA.

VHEN sommer drees shake fort deir leafs,
  Ash maids shake out deir locks,
Und singen mit de rifulets,
  Vitch ripplen round de rocks,

Und beople swarm land-outwards,
  Und cities weary men,
Hans Breitmann rode de Belgier mark
  For Spa in Les Ardennes.

Und vhen he came to Spadenland,
  He found it fein und fair,
For dey pour him out de péké schnapps,
  Dazu elixir rare;
Und mit a soldier's inshdink
  To find a shanse to shoot,
Mitout delay he fire afay
  Right in de Grande Redoute.*

De virst shot dat der Breitmann fired
  He pring de peaches down,
For he hit de double zéro mit
  A gold Napoleon.
Und ash he raked de shiners in,
  He hummed a liddle doon:
"I kess I tont try dat again,"
  Said he, dis afdernoon.

Boot vhen he coom to *rouge et noir*,
  A tear fell tripplin denn,
Id look so moosh like goot old dimes,
  To come dose games again.

* La Redoute—the gambling-room at Spa.

Yet vhen he lossed a hundred francs,
He sadly toorned afay,
"I'd rader *keep* de tiger here,
Dan vight him, any day."

Und shtanding py de daple,
He saw a French lorette
Vat porrowed shpecie all around,
Und lossed at efery bet.
"Id's all de same mit dis or dat,
Or any kind of sin,
De lorette or de rolette—bot'
Will make de money shpin."

He trinket of Le Pouhon well,
Und from La Sauveniére;
He tried it ad de Barisart,
Und auch de Géronstére.
"Dey say dat Troot' lie in a well,
So trink from all we can,
Und here we'll prove dat Troot is Health,"
Dat's so, says Breitemann.

So long in ruined Franchimont
He sat on hollowed ground,
Und dinked of Wilhelm de la Marck,
Who'd raked dat coontry round.

"Mein Gott! how id vas mofe mine heart
To read in hishdory,
Und find de scattered shinin lights
Of vellers shoost like *me!*

"Dis nople boar-pig of Ardennes,
Dis shtately Wallowin lord,
Vas make him vamous py de pen,
Und glorious py de swordt.
Und showed his hero-scholarship,
Ven he wrote to de pishop, 'Satis,
Brulabo monasterium
Vestrum, si non payatis.'

"Dey say dat in de keller here
Dere lifes a coblin briest,
Dereto a teufelsjägersmann
Vot guard a specie chest.
O if I vonce could find de vay,
Und spot.dat box of checks,
I voonder shoost how long 'twould pe
Pefore I'd twis deir necks."

Und in de Walk of Meyerbeer,
Vhere plashin brooklets ring,
He see vhere in de water wild
De wood-birds flip deir wing.

"Ash de prooklet's lost in de rifer,
  Und de rifer's lost in de sea,
Mine soul kits lost on water 'plain,'"
  Says Breitemann, says he.

Und ash he walked de Meyerbeer
  He marcked, peside de way,
A rock shoost like a wild boar's head,
  Vraie tête du sanglier.
Der Breitmann heafe a shiant sigh,
  Und say mit 'motion grand:
Von crate idée ish über all
  In dis der Schweinpig's land.

He drafel troo de Val d'Ambléve,
  He lounge de schweet Sept Heures,
He shdare indo de window-shops,
  Und see de painted ware.*
He looket at de fans und dings,
  Denn said, "To tell de trut',
Dere's painted vares more dear ash dis
  Oop shdairs in La Redoute."

* Spa is famous for painted ornamental wooden ware, such as fans and boxes.

Und sittin in de Champignon,
  Vitch rose 'neat Lofe's schweet hand,
He read in books of Marmontel,
  Of Jeannette et Lubin.
Id's nice to see Simplicitas
  Rococoed oop mit vlowers,
Und dink *soosh* virtue shdill may life
  In dis base vorldt of ours.

'Tvas here, oopon de Spadoumont
  Deir gottashe used to set;
'Tvas here they keeped von simple cow
  Likevise an lettuce-bett.
Berhaps I hafe crown vorldly since,
  Yet shdill may druly say,
Dat in mine poyhood's tays I vas
  Apout so good ash dey.

But he vot vant to see dis land,
  Und has nod time for all:
Eash woodland nook und shady brook:
  On Herr Marcette shouldt call.
For he has baintet all to live
  Vhen de drees demselfs are gone;
Und shoost so goot as artist, auch,
  Ish he bon compagnon.

Farevell, schveet Spa—dou home of vlowers
  Of ruin and of rock,
Vhere vild pirds sing und de band ish blay
  Eash tay at sefen o'clock.
If all de shbrees dat Spa has seen
  Vere melted into von
De soul vouldt reach Nirwana—lost
  In transcendental fun.

BREITMANN IN OSTENDE.

Hupsa! jonker Jan,
Die wel ruiter worden kan.

BOON tidings to der Breitmann came
  Ash he sat at table end,
Dere's right goot fisch at Blankenberghe,
  Und oysters in Ostend.
Denn to Ostland ve will reiten gaen,
  To Ostland o'er de sand,
Dou und I mit pridle drawn
  For dere ish de oyster land.

Und vhen dey shtood bei Ostersee,
  Vhere de waters roar like sin,
Dere coom five hundert fischer volk
  To dake der Breitmann in.
"Gotts doonder! Should ve doomple down
  Amoong de waters plue,
I kess you'd vant more help from me
  Dan I should vant from you!

"If you hat peen vhere I hafe peen
  Und see vot *I* hafe see,
Vhere de surf rise oop nine tausend feet,
  In de land of Nieuw Jarsie;
Und schwimmed dat surf åsh *I* hafe schwimmed,
  Peside de Jersey stran'"——
From dat day fort' de Ostland men
  Shdeered glear of der Breitemann.

Boot von ding set him shvearin so,
  I dinked he'd nefer cease,
De Ostend oysters kostet more
  In Ostend als Paris.
Hans asked an anciendt fisherman,
  To 'splain dis if he may,
Und says he, "Mijn Heer—dey're beter hier
  Als ein hundert leagues afay.

"Und as de oysters beter hier
Of course dey kostet more"——
Der Breitmann dook his bilcrim shdaff,
Und toorned him to de toor.
Says Hans, "De Vlaemsche fischermen
Can sheat de vorldt I pet,
Dey sheaten von anoder too,
All's fisch to a Dutchman's net.

"Der king peginned a palace hier,
De palace hat to shtop,
He foundt de beoples sheaten so
He gife de bildin oop.
Aldough das Leben hier ish goot,
Ad least Ostend-sibly"——
So shpoke der Breitemann und cut
Dat city py de sea.

BREITMANN IN GENT.

Wie kennt die stad waer alles nog
 Van Vlaenderens grootheid spreekt?
Waer ontrouw, valschheid en bedrog
 Van schæmte nog verbleekt?

—LEDEGANCK.

IF I hat gold, as I hafe time,
 I tells you how 'tvere shpent,
On efery year I'd shtay a week
 In Vlanderen's hoofstad, Gent.
For, oh! de sveet wild veelins,
 In dat stad do mofe me so,
Vhen I'd dink of all de clorious men
 Vot life dere long aco.

If efer man hat manly heart,
 He'd veel dat heart to beat,
Vhen mit de oldten dime of Ghent
 He valks troo efery shdreet.

Und ach! de volk are yet so goot,
It gave me soosh a pliss,
Ven I hear a bier-hous spielman sing
A melodie like dis:—

"Het was op eenen Monday,
All on a Monday free,
Dat mijnheere Jacob Van Artevelde
Unto his men said he:
He seide—'Mijn lief gesellen,
Ve all moost ride out land,
And trive our way to Bruges town,
Or Brussel in Braband.'

"Und as he oonto Brussel cam,
De meisjes sprong from bed,
Und found Mynheere Van Artevelde
Mit a cross-bolt troo his head."
Und shoost pecause dis bier-hous song
Recht troo my heartsen vent,
I feel dat I could life und die
All in de down of Gent.

Breitmann in Holland.

'S GRAVENHAGE.—THE HAGUE.

In dis boem, mein freund der Herr Breitmann hafe his fiews on art pefore-geset mit a deepness und shorthood vich is bropably oonliked in Aesthetik. Ve hafe here, within de circumcomprehensifeness of dirty-two lines, a théorie vitch—shortsomely exbressed—sends to der teufel efery dings ash vas efer gescribed pefore on kunst or art, und maket efery podics from Baumgartner doun to Fischer und Taine, look shoost like puddin-headet old gasbalgs. Boot to de boem. For de informadion of dem ash ish not gestudied art, I vould shtate dat Adriaan Brauwer (who ish as regards an unvollkomene technik de first of all Holland malers), vas nefer paint nodings boot droonken plackguards und liederlich dings, und Van Ostade und Jan Steen vas in most deir bilds a goot deal like him.

—Fritz Schwackenhammer.

HANS reitet troo de Nederland,
From Rotterdam below,
To Gravenhaag und Leyden
Und Haarlem—all a row;

He shtoodit in de galleries
  A tausend works of art;
Boot ach—der Adriaan Brauwer,
  Vent most teepest to his heart.

Und dus exglaim ber Breitmann
  In woonder-solemn shdrain,
" De cratest men vere Brauwer,
  Van Ostadé, und Jan Steen
Der Raffael vas vel enof;
  Dat ish in his shmall vay;
Boot—Gott im Himmel!—vot vas he
  Coompared mit soosh as dey?

"Shoost see dat vight of troonken boors
  Von tears de oder's goat:
Vhile de oder mit a pointet knife
  Ish goin for his troat.
Und a mädchen mit a tree-leg shtuhl
  Ish clip him on de het,
In dese higher human passion valks,
  Der Raffael's coldt und deadt.

" De more ve digs into de eart'—
  Or less ve seeks a star,—
De nearer ve to *Natur* coom,
  More panthéistich far;

To him who reads dis myst'ry right,
  Mit insbiration gifen,
Der Raffael's rollen in de dirt,
  Vhile Brauwer soars to Heafen."

BREITMANN IN LEYDEN.

'TIS shveet to valk in Holland towns
  Apout de twilicht tide,
Vhen all ish shdill on proad canals,
  Safe vhere a poat may clide.
Shdrange light on darkenin vater falls,
  In long soft lines afar,
Der abenddroth on dunkelheit,
  Vitch shows—or hides—a star.

De pridges risen all aroundt
  So quaindly, left und right,
Pedween each pridge und shattow, lies,
  A lemon of yellow light,
Und das volk a-goin ober,
  So darklin onwarts pass,
Dey look like Chinese shattows—shown
  Apofe a lookin-glass.

All shdiller grows, und shdiller,
  Sogar die efenin preeze,
Ish only heardt far ober het
  In dese long lines of drees;
A real oldt Holland feelin
  Cooms gadderin ober all,
You'd nefer dink a sturm hat peen
  Oopon dis Grand Canawl.

De nople houses!—how dey'd mofe
  An old New Yorker's heart,
Time vas—twix dese und dose at home
  You couldn't tell 'em part,
Mit crate brass knockers on de toors,
  Und parlors town so low
You see de crates a glowin prite
  O'er carbets ash you go.

Dere's comfort-full of avery dings,
  You veel it ash you look,
You knows de volks ish opulend,
  Und keep a bully cook;
Und oopon de high camine,
  Or here und dere on shelf,
Dere's Japanesisch dings in rows,
  Pe mingled oop mit delf.

Dere's noding in dis Holland life,
  Vitch seems of present day,
De fery shildren in de shdreeds
  Look quaintlich as dey blay,
De liddle rosy housemaids,
  In bicdures vell I know,
De dames und heers have all an ai·
  Of sixdy years ago.

They may dalk of anciendt hishdory
  Und for romantisch seek,
De ding dat mofes most teeply ish
  Old-vashioned—not antique.
O if you live in Leyden town
  You'll meet, if troot' pe told,
De forms of all de freunds who tied
  Vhen du werst six years old.

SCHEVENINGEN.

OR DE MAIDEN'S COORSE.

Oldt Flämisch.

HET vas Mijn Heer van Torenborg,
  Ride oud oopon de sand,
Und vait to hear a paardeken;
  Coom tromplin from de land.
He vaited vhen de boeren volk
  Vent oud oopon de plain,
He vaited dill de veary crows
  Flew nestwarts home acain.

He vaited ash de wild fox vaits
  In long-some hoonger noth,
He vaited dill de flitterin bats
  Vere plack on Abendroth.
Id's woe to watch for taily bread
  Or bide forgotten call,
Boot oh, to vait for heartsen lofe
  Ish veariest of dem all.

"O dat ish not mine laity's prooch
  Shoost now so star-like shined,
O dat ish not mine laity's haar
  Soft floatin on de wind.
Her goot crayhound mit soosh a step,
  Vas nefer vont to go,
Und dat is niet her paardeken
  Whose shtep so vell I know.

"Dat light ish speer light from a lanz
  Vich 'll part mine pody und soul,
De floatin haar is a pennon gay
  Or wafin banderol.
De crayhound ish a ploot-hound wild
  Vitch long has dracked me here,
Und het paardeken ish a var-horse
  Vot has hoonted me like deer."

Well shpoke Mijn Heer van Torenborg
  All drue vas afery wordt,
For dey bored him troo mit lanzen,
  Und dey hewed him mit de swordt.
Dey killt him armloss, harmlos;
  De plooty reiver band;
Und puried him so careloosly
  Dat his vace shtick out de sand.

Boot e'er night's plack hat toorned to red
  Or e'er de stars vere gone,
Dere came de shtep of a paardeken
  Soft tromplin, tromplin on.
A laity fair climbed off on him
  Und trip mit dainty toes:—
Boot oh, mijn Gott!—how she vas shkreem
  Ven she trot on her drue lofe's nose!

"Oh vot ish dis I trots opon?
  Ids shape fool well I know,
Der nefer yet vas flower like dis
  Dat in de garten crow.
Dere nefer yet vas fruit like dis
  Ash ripen on a dree;
Het is Mijn Heer van Torenborg
  Dat kan ik blainly see.

"Dat heerlijk nose, van Torenborg,
  Ish known of anciend dime,
'Tis writ in olten chronikel
  Und sung in minsdrel rhyme.
Und dis, de noblest of de race
  Since hisdory pegans,
Ish shtickin here—shdraighdt out de dirt,
  Shoost like some boer manns.

"Oh cuss de man dat mordered him!
  Ach, cuss him oop and down,
Ja—cuss him troo de forest roads,
  Und tamn him in de toun!
Und burn his vater und moder,
  Vhere'er deir vootshteps vall,
Mit his schwesters und his broders,
  De teufel rake dem all!

"May afery cuss dat e'er vas cusst,
  Since cussin foorst pegan;
Pe hoorled in von drementous cuss,
  Acainsdt dat nasdy man!
From de foorst crate cuss on Adam,
  To de smalles' of de crop"—
Here de tead man gafe a shifer,
  Und gry oud—"For Gott's sake—*shdop!*

"Dere's a cerdain lot of shwearin,
  Vitch anger alvays crafes;
Boot spite like dat's enof to pring
  De tead men from deir craves.
I can't lie here no longer,
  Und hear soosh pizen pain;
Und since you've shtirred me out, I kess
  I'll coom to life acain."

16

Mit von drementous shkreem of pliss,
His drue lofe shtood de shock
Den catcht him wildly py de nose,
"Ach Torenborg—lev'st du nock!
Ach ja—du aint'st nod tead yet!
Dere's life shdill lef' pehind,
Gott pless de chance dat lef' dy nose,
Shdill wafin in de wind."

Mit hands all ofer diamonds,
She loosed de sand apout,
Mit an oyster-shell so wildly
She digged her lofer out.
"Und now dou'rt in free air, lofe!
Who warst shoost now in sand!
Dere vas'nt ish a nicer man,
In all de Nederland!"

Vhere vas dit liedeken written,
Vhere vas dit liedeken sing,
Dat had gedone Hans Breitmann,
In de town of Schevening!
'Tvas written ober Rheinwein,
'Tvas written ober bier—
Und wer das lied gesungen hat,
Gott geb ihm ein glucklich's jahr.*

* And to him who sung this song,
God give a happy year.

BREITMANN IN AMSTERDAM.

TO Amsterd—m came Breitmann
  All in de Kermes tide;
Yonge Maegden allegader
  Filled de straat on afery side.
De meisjes in de straaten
  Vere tantzin alle nacht long;
Dere vas kissen, dere vas trinken,
  Mit a roar of Holland song.

Who went into de straaten
  Ven de sonn had gone his day,
De Dootch gals quickly grapped him,
  Und tantzed him wild avay.
Dere was der Prinz von Capua,
  Who fell among dese wags;
Dey tantzed him off in a carmagnole,
  Und sent him home in rags.

Und den at afery gorner,
  So peaudifool to see,
De volk was bilin dough-nuts,
  Or else was fryin tea.

Und Kermes cakes mit boetry,
  Vitch land-volk dinks a dreat,
Mit all of Barnum's blayed out shows
  In dents along de shdreet.

Id pring de tears to Breitmann's eyes,
  To find in many a shtand
Vot oft he'd baid a quarder for
  To see in a distand land.
De Aztec dwins und de Siamese.
  (Dough soom vere a wachsen sham);
Mit de Beardet Frau und de Bear Woman—
  All here in Amsterdam.

De fashion here in Nederland
  Ish not vot you'd soopose,
Mit oos, men bays de vomens,
  Boot de Dootch gals hires deir beaux!
Dey hire dem for de season,
  Und pecause moosh rain ish fell,
Dey alvays bays a higher brice,
  For a man mit an umberell.

Und dere was Nord Hollander maids,
  So woonderfool to see,
Mit caps of gold und goldne pins,
  Und quaint orféverie.

Likewise de Zeeland boersmen,
  Mit silber bootons gay;
Und silber belts, und silber knives,
  Mijn Gott!—how sdrange vere dey!

But dough de men wore silber gear,
  Und de vrouws in gold were tall,
De gals vere gabblin all de dimes,
  Und de men said noding at all.
Dey say dat sbeech is silbern,
  Boot silence golden pe,
Dat aint de vay dey vork id here,"
  Said Breitemann, said he.

Goot Gott! how Breitmann vent it,
  In moonlighdt or in rain;
Den vakened to Schied—m it,
  Ven de mornin peamed again.
For to solfe von awfool broplem,
  He vas efer shdill incline;
If—den wijn is beter als de min,*
  Or—de min doet veel meer als de wijn.

* If wine is better than loving,
Or if love doth much more than wine.

Dwo weeks der Breitmann studiet,
Vile he vent it on de howl,
He shpree so moosh to find de troot,
Dat he lookt like a bi-led owl.
Den he say, "Ik wil honor Bacchus,
So long as ik leven shall;
Boot not so moosh vercieren
As to blace him ofer all.

De rose of lofe is lofely
In zomer ven it plow;
De bush shdill gifes a bromise,
In winter mid de shnow;
Ja, als de bloeme is geplukt,
En van den steel genomen,*
Ve know de peautiful vill life,
Till zomer is gekomen.

Boot oh dose vas arch-heafenly dimes,
Ven by mine lofe I sat;
Und see de maedchen pring de grapes,
Und crash dem in a vat.

* Yes, when the flower is plucked,
And taken from the stem.

Und ven her glances unto mine
  In plessfool ropture toorn;
I dink dere ne'er vas no dwo crapes
  Like dem plue eyes of hern.

Wat is soeter als de trinken,*
  Ja—niet kan beter zyn.
Niet is soeter as de minne,
  It smackt nog beter als wijn.
Es giebt nichts wie die Mädchen,
  Es gibt nichts wie das Bier,
Wer liebt nicht alle beide,
  Wird gar kein Cavalier.

O vot ve vant to quickest come,
  Ish dat vot's soonest gone.
Dis life ish boot a passin from
  De efer-gomin-on.
De gloser dat ve looks ad id,
  De shmaller it ish grow;
Who goats und spurs mit lofe und wein,
  He makes it fastest go.

* What is sweeter than this drinking?
  Yes—naught can better be.
Naught is sweeter, though, than loving;
  It tastes better than wine to me.
There's nothing like the maidens,
  There's nothing like good beer,
And he who does not love them both
  Can be no cavalier.

Breitmann in Germany.

BREITMANN AM RHEIN.—COLOGNE.

HOW wunderschön das Vaterland
  In audumn-life abbears;
Vot rainpows gild ids vallies crand,
  Ven seen troo vallin tears.
Und VON I'll creet mit sang und klang,
  Und drown in goldnen wein;
Old Deutschland's cot her sohn again:
  Hans Breitmann's on der Rhein.

Und doughts ish schwell dat mighdy heart,
  Too awfool for make known;
Ven dey shunt him from de railroat car
  Und tropped him in Cologne.
De holy towers of de dome
  Cleam, twilicht-veiled, afar;
Und like some lonely bilgrim's pipe,
  Dim shines de efenin star.

Hans look to find his baggage check,
  Und see dat all ish shdraighdts,
Denn toorn him to de city toors,
  "Mein nadife land—wie gehts?"
Boot *dat's* vot all who read may run—
  Fool blainly armies write;
Id's ofer all half Shermany,
  Set down in Black and White.

Oh, Black and White! O Weiss and Schwarz!
  Vot dings ish dis to see?
I vonder vot in future years
  Your mission ish to pe?
Also in crate America
  We had soosh colors too!
Die Färb' sind mir nicht unbekannt*—
  Id's shoost *tout comme chez nous.*

Next tay to de Cathedral
  He vent de dings to view,
Und found it shoost drei thaler cost
  To see de sighds all troo.
"Id's tear," said Hans; "boot go ahet,
  I'fe cot de cash all right;
Boot id's queer dat's only Protestands
  Vot mosdly see de sighdt!

* The colours are not unknown to me.

"Im Mittelalter I hafe read
  De shoorsh vas alvays sure—
An open bicdure gallerie,
  Und book for all de poor.
Boot now de dings is so arrange
  No poor volk can get in;
We Yankees und de Englisch are
  Pout all ash shbends de tin.

"I shmiles like Mephistopheles
  In shoorshes ven I see
Poor Catholics vollerin round apout
  To shdeal a sighdt—troo ME!
Dey peep und creep roundt chapel gates,
  Boot soon kits trofe afay,
Dey gross demselfs, und make a brayer—
  Boot den dey cannot bay!

"Dese Deutsche sacrisdans might learn
  More goot in Italy,
Where beoples bays shoost half de brice,
  For ten dimes more to see,
De volk vot dink I shbeak sefere
  Apout dese Küster vays,
May read vot Mr. Bädeker
  In his Belgine Hand Buch says."

Und valkin oop und town de down
  Von ding vas shdill de same:
Shoost ash of oldt he saw de shpread
  Of Jean Farina's name.
He find it nort', he find it sout',
  He find it eferyvhere;
Dere vas no house in all Cologne
  Boot J. M. F. vas dere.*

De best Cologne in all Cologne
  I'll shwear for cerdain sure,
Ish maket in de Jülichsplatz
  Und dat at Numero Four.
Boot of dis Cologne in Jülichsplatz
  Let dis pe undershtood,
Dat some of id ish foorst-rate pad,
  Vhile some ish foorst-rate good.

Boot von ding drafellers moost opserve,
  Dis treadful trut I dells,
Fast ash dis Farinaceous crowd
  So vast hafe grown the schmells—

* "Ils etaient deux alors ; ils sont mille aujourd hui.
Sur ces temps primitifs le doux progrés a lui,
Et chacque jour le Rhin vers Cologne charrie
De nombreux Farinas, tous 'seul,' tous 'Jean Marie.'"
Le Maout, "*Le Parfumeur*," cited by Eugene Rimmel in *Le Livre des Parfums*, Paris, 1870.

Dose awfool schmells in gass' und strass'
  Vitch mofe crate Coleridge squalm:
If *so* he wrote, vot vouldt he write
  Apout dem now, py tam?

Of all de schmells I efer schmelt,
  Py gutter, sink, or well,
At efery gorner of Cologne
  Dere's von can peat dat schmell.
Vhen dere you go you'll find it so,
  Don't dake de ding on troost;
De meanest skunk in Yankee land
  Vould die dere of disgoost.

Boot noding dinked der Breitmann
  Of schmutz or idle schein,
Vhen he sat in Abendämmerung
  Und looket owd on der Rhein
Im goldnen gleam—vhile pealin far
  Rang shlow, shveet kloster bells,
Und in de dim, plue peaudiful,
  Rose distant Drachenfels.

Dey trinket lieb Liebfrauenmilch,
  So pure ash voman's trut';
De singed de songs of Shermany,
  De songs of Breitmann's yout'.

De songs mit tears of vanished years,
  Made peaudiful in wein.
Dus endet out de firster tay
  Of Breitmann on der Rhein.

AM RHEIN.—No. II.

IM KAHN.

Were diu werlt alle min,
Von deme mere unze an den Rin,
Des wolt ih mih darben,
Daz diu dame von Engellant
Lege an minen armen.

—*Carmina Burana.*

AM Rhein! Acain am Rheine!
  In boat oopon der Rhein!
De castle-bergs soft goldnen
  Im Abendsonnenschein,
Mit lots of Rudesheimer,
  Und saitenklang und sang,
Und laties singin lieder,
  Ash ve go sailin 'long.

Und von fair Englisch dame
  Vas dere, so wunderscheen;
Vene'er der Breitmann saw her,
  Id made his heartsen pain.
Oh, dose long-tailed veilchen Augen,
  Vitch voke soosh hopes und fears,
Deir shape vas nod like almonds,
  Boot more like fallin tears.

Und shpecdagles were o'er dem,
  De glass of pince-nez kind,
In mercy to de beoples,
  Less dey pe shdrucken blind.
Und gazin in dem glasses,
  Reflected he pehold
De Rhine, mit all de shdeam-poats,
  Und crags in Sonnengold.

De signs upon de bier-haus!
  De gals a-washin close;
De wein-garts on de moundain,
  Like heafenly shdairs in rows;
De banks, basaltic-paven,
  Like bee-hife cells to view;
A donkey shtandin on dem,
  Likevise her lofer too.

All dis oopon dos glasses,
  Vas blainly to pe seen;
One saw whate'er vas nodiced,
  Py de schöne Engländrinn.
Boot oh! de fery lofe-most
  Of all dat lofe-most pe
Her own plue veilchen Augen—
  Herself she couldt not see.

So ist es in dis Leben;
  For beaudy oft we spied,
Nor know de cratest peaudy
  Ish in our soul inside.
Mein Gott! Vot himmlisch shplendor
  Vas seen mitout an toubt,
If some crate bower supernal
  Vas toorn life insite out!

Und gazin long on Natur,
  Und gazin long on Man,
Shdill all dings glite vorüber,
  Ash since de vorldt pegan:
Ash in laity's glasses,
  Ve see dem bassin py;
Yet veel a soul beneat' dem,
  A schweet eternal eye.

O schöne Englisch maiden
  Mit honey colored hair,
Dat flows ash if a bienen korb
  Had got oopsettet dere—
Und all de schweetness of your soul
  Vas dripplin from your brain!
Oh shall I efer meet mit dir
  Oopon dis eart' acain?

O Englisch engel maiden!
  O schveet betaubend dofe!
O Rheinwein und cigarren!
  O luncheon, mixed mit lofe;
O Drachenfels und Nonnenwerth!
  O Liebeslust und pein!
Dus ents de second chapterlet,
  Of Breitmann on der Rhein.

AM RHEIN.—No. III.

NONNENWERTH.

(Alt Deutsch.)

HE shtood peside de Kloster-place,
Oopon de Rheinisch shore,
Und dere he saw a lofely face,
He'd seen in treams pefore.

"Feinslieb, und will'st dou go mit me?
Feinslieb, make no delay;
For rocks ish shdeep und vales ish teep,
Und dings ish in de way."

"Und oh! how can I go mit dir,
Or flyen out of land?
Der bischof holts me py de law,
Der Rheingraf by der hand.

"Liebsherz, if dou could'st landwarts gehn,
I'd follow willingly;
Boot we are leafs, und shdrong's de shdem
Vitch pinds oos to de dree."

"Der briest who helt dee py de law
 Ish now a broken man;
Der Rheingraf who vouldt marry dee
 Ish in der Kaisar's ban.

"Und if de Kloster-beoples here
 Vill shdop your goin to town,
Bei Gott! I'll burn von half of dem,
 De oder half I'll trown!

"Denn linger not to back dy drunk,
 Boot led our lofe hafe vings;
Dere's milliners in fair Cologne,
 Vill make you avery dings."

She toorn her eyes im mondenschein,
 She schmile so heafenly:
"Dear lofe, so shendle und so goot!
 I'll cut away mit dee.

"Und do not kill de Kloster-volk,
 'Tvouldt only bring tiscrace:
Dough if I had de abbess here,
 Lort! how I'd slap her vace!"

De moonlighdt blayed oopon de drees,
 It shined oopon de blain,
Two forms rode in de mitnight woods,
 Und nefer coomed again.

Breitmann in Munich.

GAMBRINUS.

"Vot ish Art? Id ish *somedings to drink*, objectively fore-gebrought in de Beaudiful. Doubtest dou?—denn read, ash *I* hafe read, de Dyonisiacs of Nonnus, und learn dat de oop-boorstin of infinite worlds into edernal Light und mad goldnen Lofeliness—yea of *dein own soul*—is typifide only py de CUP. Vot!—shdill skebdigal? Tell me denn, O dou of liddle fait, vere on eart ish de kunst obtain ids highest form if not in a BIERSTADT?* Ha! ha! I poke you *dere!*

Caupo Recauponatus, MS. by Fritz Schwackenhammer, *olim canditatus theologiæ* at Tübingen, shoost now lagerbierwirth in St. Louis. (Dec. 1869.)

Cerevisia bibunt homines
Animalia ceteræ fontes.

I.

IN a field of goldnen parley
Goot King Gambrinus shlept,
Und treamin' pout de dursty volk,
Dey say he gried und vept.

**Bierstadt*—Herr Schwackenhammer had evidently here in view, not only the American artist BIERSTADT, but also the great city of Munich, specially famous for its manufacture of beer.

"In all mine land of Nederland,
  Dere crows no mead or wein,
Und wasser I couldt nefer get
  Indo dis troat of mein.

"Now hear me on, ye headen gotts!
  Und all de Christian too;
Der Bacchus und der Shoopider,
  Und Màrie tressed in plue!
Und mighdy Thor, der donner gott,
  Und any else dat be!
Der von as helps me in dis Noth,
  His serfant I will pe."

Und ash dis sinfull headen
  All in de parley lay,
Dere coom in tream an angel
  Who soft dese worts tid say:
"Stay oop, dou boor Gambrinus!
  For efen all aroundt
Im parley vhere dou shleepest,
  Some dings goot to trink ish found.

"Im parley vhere dou shleepest
  Dere hides a trink so clear,
Dat men will know zukunftig—
  Ash porter—ale—or bier."

Und denn in Nederlandisch
  He put de könig troo,
Und gafe him—allwhile treaming—
  De recipé to prew.

Oop rose der goot Gambrinus,
  Und shook him in de sun:
"Go vay, ye sinfool headen gotts!
  Mit you its out und done!
Ye'fe left me mit mine beoples
  In error und in durst,
Till in our treadful tryness,
  Ve tont know vitch is wurst."

Dat vas der goot Gambrinus
  Oonto his palac't vent,
Und loafers troo de Nederland
  To all his lordts he sent.
"Leave Odin—or you lose your hets!"
  De order vas sefere,
Yet tinged mit mildness, for he sent
  De recipé for bier.

O den a merry sound vas heardt
  Of bildin troo de land,
Und de kirchen und de braweries
  Vent oop on efery hand;

For de masons dey vere hart at vork,
  Und trinkin hart at dat,
Und some hat bricks mitin de hods,
  Und some mitin deir hat.

Dey prew it in de Nederland,
  Dey prew it on de Rhine;
Boot in de oldt Bavarian land,
  Dey make it shdrong und fein.
Und he dat trinks in Munich,
  Ash all goot vellers know,
Has got somedings to dink apout,
  Vherefer he may go.

II.

Hafe you heardt of Köng Gambrinus?
  If you hafen't id vas gueer,
For he vas de first erfinder
  Und de holy saint of bier.
Und his bortrait, mit a sceptre,
  Fery peaudifool to see,
Hangs on afery lager-bier house,
  In de land of Germanie.

Efery vhere de whole world ofer,
  Deutschers paint him on de sign,
As a broof dat dey are dealin
  In de Bok und Lager line.

Crown und bier-mug, robe und ermine;
  German signs of empire, dese,
Mit a long white beard a fallin'
  Fery nearly to his knees.

Vonce dis bier-saint, pright und early,
  Rose from bett und vent his vay,
To a dark mysderious gastle,
  Vhere his lager-donjon lay.
Vhile de lark's first song vas ringin',
  Und die roses shone in dew,
Den his soul vas shoost in order
  To enshoy de early brew.

Deeply, awfooly he schwilled it,
  Till de vaults seem toornin round;
Und vhile tipsy—*over* tips he—
  In he falls—und dere is trowned.
Yet vhile goorglin in de bier-fass,
  Biously he gafe his soul:
"Gott verdammich! Donnerwetter!
  Himmels sacrament-a-mol!"

Dere dey found der köng "departed,"
  Not mitout his stir-up cup:
Moosh dey woonderd dat he berishet
  Vhen he might hafe troonk it oop·

Or dat his long peard vitch floatet
Fool a yard on efery side,
Hadn't buoyed him from destrugdion :—
Dus der beer-dead monarch died.

BREITMANN IN FRANKFORT-ON-THE-MAIN.

Sankt Martin war ein frommer Mann
Trank gerne *Cerevisiam*,
Und hatt er kein *Pecuniam*
So liess er seinen *Tunicam*.

(COMMENT BY HERR SCHWACKENHAMMER.)

VONCE oopon a dimes in Frankfort der Herr Breitemann exsberiencet an interfal pedween de periot ven he hat gespent de last remiddance he hat become from home, und de arrifal of de succedin wechsel, or bill of exghange—und, in blain derms, was hard up. Derefore he vent to dat goot relation who may pe foundt at den or fifdeen per cent. all de worlt ofer,—"mine Onkel,"—und poot his tress-goat oop de shpout for den florins. No sooner vas dis done, dan dere coomed an infitation from de English laity in whom he vas so moosh mit lofe in betaken, to geh mit her to a ball-barty.

Awful bad vas he veel, und sot apout tree hours mitout sayin nodings, und denn wafin his hand, boorst out mit de vollowin version of dat peaudiful lied by Wilhelm Caspary:—

"Mein Frack ist im Pfand-haus."

Mine tress-goat is shpouted, mine tress-goat aint hier,
Vhile you in your ball-ropes go splurgin, mein tear!
To barties mit you I'm infitet you know,
Boot my pest coat ish shpouted—mine poots are no go.
To hell mit mine Onkel—dat rasgally knafe!
Dis pledgin und pawnin has mate me his slafe!
Ven I dink of his sign-bost, den dree dimes I bawl,
Vhile mine plack pants hang lonely und dark on de wall,

Goot night to dee fine lofe—so lofely und rich,
Mein tress-goat ish shpouted—gon-fount efery stitch!
I dinks dat olt Satan troo all mine affairs,
Lofe, business, und fun, has peen sewin his tares,
My tress-goat ish shpouted—mine tress-goat aint here,
While you in your glorie go shinin, mein tear,
Und de luck of der teufel ish loose ofer all,
Vhile my black pants hang lonely und dark on de wall.

Dis *four-goin* song vas over-set by der Hans Breitmann from de German of Wilhelm Caspary, whose lyric vas a barody on a dranslation made indo Deutsch by Freiligrath from anoder boem py Sir Waldherr Scott, vich Sir Waldherr vas kit de idée of from an oldt Scottish ballad vitch pegin mit de vorts—

"My hearts in de Hielands, mein hearts ish nae hier,
Mein hearts in de Hielands, in wilden revier;
It hoonts for de shtag, und id hunts for de reh,
Mein hearts ist im Hochland wo immer ich geh."

Dis is de orginal Scotch, so goot as I can mineself rememper it. Ven I vas dell der Herr Karl Blind pout dis intercommixture of preplexified dransitions from Scotch to English, and dence into German, and dereafter into a barody, vitch vas be done ofer again indo Herr Breitmann's own slanguage, he sait it vas a Rattenkönig—a phrase too familiar to mine readers to require any wider complication.*

*Rattenkönig, or Rat-king, is a term applied in German to a droll mixture of incidents or details. It is derived from an extraordinary story of twelve rats, with one (their king) in the centre, which were found in a nest with their tails grown together, firmly as the ligament which connects the Siamese Twins.

Breitmann in Italy.

BREITMANN IN ROME.

DERE'S lighds oopon de Appian,
Dey shine de road entlang;
Und from ein hundert tombs dere brumms
A wild Lateinisch song;
It rings from Nero's goldnen haus;
Evoe!—here he coom!
Fly oud, ye mœnads, from your craves!—
Hans Breitmann's got to Rome!

For vhile de lamp holts oud to purn,
Or von goot shpark ish dere,
Dere's hopes for all of dem whose lives
Ish doun in Lemprière.
Von real, *shenuine* heathen
Is coom at last to home;
Ye shleepin gotts, lift oop your hets—
Hans Breitmann lifes in Rome!

Silenus mit der Hercules,
  Dere-to der Maia's sohn,
Ish all unite in Breitmann
  To make a stunnin one.
Frau Venus mit de Bacchanals
  Ist shmile to see him come;
De Vesta only toorn her pack
  Vhen Breitmann kit to Rome.

He vented to de Vacuum,
  Vhere de Bope ish keep his bulls;
Boot couldn't vind dem, dough he heardt
  Dat all de blace vas fools.
Dere ish here and dere some *ochsen*,
  Right manivest I see;
Boot de bools all comes from Irish priests,
  Said Breitmann, said he.

Und goin' py de Vacuum,
  Und passin' troo de yard;
Mein Gott! how vas he stoomple, vhen
  He see he Schweitzer guard,
Mit efery kinds of colors tresst,
  Like shtreamers in de van.
"Hans Wurst ist stets ein Deutscher g'west,"
  Das marked der Breitmann.

Und dus replied an guartsmann—
"I shoys to see you here:
Ich bin dem Bapst sei Laibgaertner.
Dazu a halberthier.
Dis purpur kleid of yellow-plue
Vas made, ash I hafe heard,
Py von Hans Michel Angelo,
Der tailor of our guard.

"Ve're shoost von hoondert dirty strong,
Ve list for twenty year:
De serfice ist not pad, boot dis—
Verdamm das Römisch bier!
For ven mit *birra gazzosa*
A maiden fills my glass,
She might ash vell gife gift ash say—
'Feinsleib, ich schenk dir dass!'"

Und dus rebly der Breitmann:—
"Un Tedesco Italianazato,
Ein Deutscher toorned Italian, ish
Il diavolo in carnato.
Your clothes are like infernal flames,
Dey burn my fery soul;
Boot to-night we'll trink togedder—nun
Lieb' landsmann lebe wohl!"

At de Sherman artisds' festa,
  Vhere all vas pright und fair,
'Tvas fairer und more prighterfull
  Vhen Breitmann enter dere.
Und der vaiters in de Greco
  (So long he trinked und sot)
Vas called him L'Ubbriacone—
  'Tvas de name der Breitmann got.

He saw a veller in de shtreet,
  Vot sell some friction-matches;
De kind dey call Infallible,
  For dey *blazes* ven you *scratches*.
Dey dragged him off to brison,
  Und tied him mit a rope;
For in Rome dere's nix Infallible,
  Dey said, excebt de Bope.

Hans see de crate Prometheus,
  In Corsini's gallery hang;
He tought apout de matches,
  Und it made his heart go bang.
It's risk to carry light apout,
  Too cheap for efery man;
How de Lucifers is fallen!*
  Ita dixit Breitemann.

* "Lucifers." The first name applied in America to friction matches and one still used by many people.

He got among de Bope's Zouaves,
  Dey trinked from morn to night;
Den frolicked *colle belle*
  Ontil de shky crew pright.
It blease der Breitmann vonderfool,
  And dus he often say:
"*Zouaviter in modo* ish
  Der real Roman way."

Boot oh, his heart burned vild mit fire,
  His eyes gefilled mit tears,
At de gotts in efery bilder saal,
  Mit goats' legs, tails, und ears.
Und he sopped—"Ach liebes Deutschland,
  Bist here on every hand?
Was machst du Mephistophelés
  So weit im Wälschen Land?"

Boot de wood-nymphs boorst out laughin,
  Der Garten-gott dere to,
Und sait—"Oldt Hans! vile you're apout
  Ve nefer can look blue."
Den Pan blay on his Syrinx,
  To de tune of Mary Blane,
"Don't gry pecause ve're out of town,
  Ve're coming pack again.

"Von day you got de yolk und vhite,
De next day only shells;
Von day dey holts a council,
Und de next day—'someding else!'
Id's bopes und kings, und gotts and dings,
Oopon dis eartly ball;
Boot for *me* id's all von frolic,
Und a high oldt carnival!

"Rise oop, dou Odin trafeler,
Und toorn dee to de Nort,
Wherefrom, as Bible dells dee,
Crate efil shall come fort.
Dere is mutterins in Ravenna,
Und ere long dere'll come a turn,
A real hell-bender from de land
Of Dieterich von Bern.

"Und ven der Breitmann's prototype,
Der Fictoor Manuel,
Cooms tromplin, tromplin troo de fern,
To give dis coontry hell.
Und ven in La Comarca,
Der is shtorm in all de air,
"Dy Gotts vill gife dee vork, mein Sohn,
Hans Breitmann shall be dere!"

For a yar will nod be ofer
  Pefore de Fräntsch will run,
Und de game at last be ented,
  Und Italy pe *won*.
Und denn in roarin battle,
  For hishtory so grand,
Dy banner'll lead de Uhlan spears,
  All in de Frankenland.

LA SCALA SANTA.

"Robusti sono i fatti."
Discorso del Terremoto, del S. Alessandro Sardo. Venetia, A.D. 1586.

IN San Gianni Lateran,
Dey've cot a flight of shdairs,
More woonderful ash nefer vas,
As Latin pooks declares.
For you kits your sins forgifen,
If you glimes dem knee py knee;
It's such a gitten up a stairs,
I nefer yet did see.

Now as Breitmann vas a vaitin
Among some demi reps,
Ascensionem expectans,
To see dem glime de steps,
Dere came a sinful scoffer,
Who his mind had firmly set
To go dem holy sdairs afoot,
Und do it on a bet!

Boot shoost as he vas startet,
  To make dis sassy go,
Der Breitmann caught him py de neck,
  Und tripped him off his toe!
Und den dere come de skience,
  A la prenez gardez vous;
For he bung his eye and bust his shell,
  Und shplit his noshe in dwo.

De briest vere so astonish,
  To see him lam de man,
Dat dey shvore a holy miracle
  Vas vork by Breitemann.
Says Breitmann, "I'm a heretic,
  But dis you may pe bound,
No chap shall mock relishious dings
  Vhile I'm a bummin round.

"Und you owes me really noding,
  For as I'll plainly show:
At last I've found out someding
  Vot I alfays vant to know.
Und now dat I have found it,
  In de newspapers I'll brag:
Evviva! Ho trovato,
  Vot means a Scala-Wag." *

* *Scalawag*—An American word, of very doubtful origin, signifying a low, worthless fellow.

BREITMANN INTERVIEWS THE POPE.

"Altri beva il Falerno, altri la Tolfa.

. . . .

Toscana re, dite
Pria ch'io parli dite."

Bacco in Toscano, di Francesco Redi.

"Si regressum feci metro
Retro ante, ante retro—
Quid si graves sunt acuti?
Si accentus fiant muti?
Quid si placide, plene, plane
Fregi frontem Prisciani?—
Sat est Verbum declinavi
Titubo-titubas-titubavi."

Barnabæ Itinerarium. London, 1716.

VON efenin ash der Breitmann vent from his weinhaus vinkin,
So peepy mit Falernian vitch he vas starkly trinkin,
He found his hut and goat was gone,—dey'd dook em oud for dryin,—
Und in deir blace a priester hut und priester mantel lyin.

Der Breitmann poot de triangel oopon his het, and whistled,
Den rop de cloak around his form, and down de Corso mizzled.
De beoples gazed mit staunischment as bey dem he go vheelin,
He look ganz *oltra tramontane*, so twisty vas his reelin.

Next tay *in Vaticano*, while he shtared at frescoes o'er him
Hans toorned und mit amazemend saw der Pabst vas shoost pefore him!
Down on his knees der Breitmann vent—for so de law is teaches;
He proke two holes in de bavement—und likevise shblit his preeches.

"Ego video," says de Bope—"tu es antistes ex Almania,
Est una mala gente et corrupta con insania,
Un fons hereticorum et malorum tut terribile,
Perche non vultis che ego—il Papa—sei infallibile."

"Sit verbo venia," said Hans, "permitte, Sancte Pater.
Num verum est ut noster *rum* gemixta est mit water?
In cœlis wo die götter live, non semper est sereno,
Nor de wein ash goot ash decet in each *spaccio di vino.*

"Sunt mihi multi fratres qui si denkunt ut dicisti,
Ego kickerem illos, validê, per sanguine de Christi!
In nostro monasterio si habemus nostrum rentum
Contra infallibilità non curamus rubrum centum.*

"Vigintia nostrorum nuper convenere,
In quodam capitulo, simul et dixere;
Papa vult Concilium in Romam tenere,
Quid debemus super hoc ipsi respondere?"†

* "If we can in our monastery collect our rents, we do not care a red cent for infallibility."

† This verse is parodied from the lines of a ribald old Latin song, "Viginti Jesuiti nuper convenêre."

Et dixit noster presul, "Es ist mir omnis unus,
Si Papa est infalliblis, tanquam non sum jejunus,
Si Nonus est Pius aut Pius est Nonus—
Diabolus curat. Non accipio dieser onus.

"Si possum me jacĕre circum vitrum Rhenovini*
Es ist mir wurst si Papa est originis divini:
Deus se fecit olim homo, et nahm das irds'che
Leben,†
Et nunc Papa noster will sich selbst zum Gott
erheben.

* "If I could throw myself outside of, or around, a glass of Rhenish wine." "If I could see a glass of whiskey," said an American, "I'd throw myself outside of it mighty quick." Since writing the above, I have seen the expression thus given in a copy of *La Belle Suavage.—Bill of the Play, London, June* 27, 1870.

"Nay these natives—simple creatures—
Had resolved that for the future
Each his own canoe would paddle,
Each his own hoe-cake would gobble,
And *get outside his own whiskey*."

† "Deus se fecit olim homo," &c. A very curious epigram to this effect was placed upon "Pasquin" while the writer was in Rome, during the past winter. It was as follows:—

"Perchè Eva mangio il pomo
Iddio per riscattarci si fece uomo,
Ed ora il Nono Pio
Per mantenerci schiavi, si fa Dio."

Ita dixit Breitmann et sanctus Pater respondit:
Me piace semper intendere tutto cio che l'on dit,
Sed tu dic mihi la sua ragione:
Tu non homo natus es, solus mangiar maccheroni.

"Tonitrus et cespes!" dixit Johanes Breitmann.
"Si veritatem cupies, tunc ego sum der right man;
Percute semper ferrum dum caldum est et *malle-able*,
Nunc est tuum tempus te facere *infallible*.

"In nostra America quum Præses decet abire,
Die ultimo fecit omne quod posset imaginire.
Appointet ambasciatores et post-magistros,
Consules et alios, per dextros et sinistros.

"Quum Rex Bomba ista Neapolit—anus,
Compulsus fuit to shin it—ut dixit Africanus—
Fecit ultimo die ducos et countos, vanus.
(Inter alios McCloskey, tuus Hibernicus chamberlanus.)*

"Et quia tu es; ut credo; ultimus Poporum,
Facis bene devenire, quod dicitur High Cockalorum—

* M'Closky. An Irish adventurer, admirably depicted by Mr. Charles Lever.

Sei magnissimus *toad in the puddle*, ite caput,
magnamente;
Et ERITIS SICUT DEUS, nemine contradicente!

"Unus error solus, Sancte Pater commisisti.
Quia primus *infallible* non te proclamavisti,
Nam nemo audet dicere: Papa fecit quod non
est bonus.
Decet semper jactare super *alios* probandi onus.

"Conceptio Immaculata, hoc modo fixisti,
Et nemo audet dicere unum verbum, de isti:
Non vides si infallibilis es, et vultis es exdare,*
Non alius sed *tu* solus hanc debet proclamare."

"Figlio mio," dixit Papa; "Tu es homo mirablis,
Tua verba sunt mi dulcior quam ostriche cum
Chablis
In tutta Roma, de Alemania gente,
Non ho visto uno con si grande mente.

"Vero benedetto es—eris benedictus,
Tibi mitterem photographiam in quo sum depic-
tus.
Tu comprendes situatio—il punto et gravamen.
Sunt pauci clerici ut te. Nunc dico tibi.—Amen!"

* Do you not see that if you are infallible, and wish to give it out.

HANS BREITMANN AT A PICNIC.

DE picknock oud at Spraker's wood:—
Id melt de soul und fire de plood.
Id sofly slid from cakes und cream;
Boot busted oop on brandy shdeam.

Mit stims of tender craceful ring,
De gals begoon a song to sing;
A bland mildt lied of olden dime—
Deutsch vas die doon, und Deutsch de rhyme.

Wi's uff der Stross' wenn's finschter ischt,
Und niemond in der Goss, mehr ischt,
Nur Schöne Mädel wolle mer fonga,
Wie es gebil'te Leut' verlonga.

At de picknock oud in Spraker's Wood,
De bier was soft—de gals were good:
Oondil von feller, vild und rasch,
Called out for a Yankee brandy-smash!

A crow vot vas valkin on de vall,
Fell dead ven he hear dis Dootchmann call;
For he knew dat droples coom, py shinks!
Ven de Dootch go in for Yankee drinks.

De Dootch got ravin droonk ash sin,
Dey smash de windows out und in;
Dey bust und bang de bar-room ein,
Und call for a bucket of branntewein.

Avay, avay, demselfs dey floong,
Und a wild infernal lied dey sung:
'Tvas, "Tam de wein, and cuss de bier!
Ve tont care nix for de demprance here!

"O keep a pringin juleps in,
Und baldface corn dat burn like sin;
Mit apple tods und oldt shtone fence,
Ve'll all get corned ere ve go hence!"

Dey dash deir glasses on de cround,
Und tanz dill 'tvas all to brick-duss ground.
Ven dey hear von man had a ten-dollar note,
De crowd go dead for dat rich man's troat.

A demperance chap vot coomed dere in,
Vent squanderin out mit his shell bust in;
"It's walk your chalks, you loost your chance,
Dis vot de call der Dootchman's dance."

Boot ven de law, mit his myrmidon,
Vas hear of dese Dootchmen's carryins-on,
Dey sent bolicemen shtern und good,
To *pull* dose Dootch in Spraker's Wood.

De Dootch vas all gone roarin mad,
Und trinked mit Spraker all dey had;
Dey shpend 'nuf money to last deir life,
And each vas tantzin mit anoder man's wife.

Dey all cot poonish difers vays,
Some vent to jug for dirty tays;
Und de von dat kilt de demperance man
Vas kit from de Alderman repriman.

Und dus it ran:—"A warnin dake,
For you mighdt hafe mate soom pig mishdake
Now how vouldt you hafe feeled, py shing!
If dat man hat peen in de whiskey ring?

"Since you votes mine dicket, of course you know,
I'm pound to led you shlide und go.
Boot nefer on whiskey trink your fill,
For you Dootchmen don't know who to kill."

Now Deutschers all—on dis warning dink,
Und don't get troonk on Yankee trink,
For neider you, or anoder man,
Can pe hocks like de New York rowdies can.

So trink goot bier, mit musik plest,
For if you tried your level best,
You can't be plackguarts—taint in de plood:
Dus endet de shdory of Spraker's Wood.

Breitmann as a Trumpeter.

DE land mit snow fur is bedecket,
  Avery dree is ge-dresst like a queen;
Dark leafs shtickin out troo de whiteness
  Like plack dails on a proud hermeline.
Und ofer der scene dere coom reiten
  Uhlanen so sholly und gay,
Mit ter ron dirry don dy ron day ne',
  Und a ron dy ron dy ron dé!

Dere's a word in a hoory gespoken,
  Und off in a gallop dey're gone:
De lances pend forvarts like mast-tops,
  Of pirates py dempests plown on.
For dey hear de Vengeurs are pefore dem,
  Und dey skurry to trive dem avay,
Mit ter ron de ron dy ron day ne',
  Und a ron dy ron don dy ron dé!

Dey boorst like a bom on de Fräntshmen;
  Boot der Hans as mit reason pereft,
Goed reiten avay from de pattle,
  Und circled around to de left,
Vhere dere shtood a Französisch trompéter,
  A plowin und pipin avay,
Mit his ron dirry don dirry day neh,
  Und don dirry don dirry dé!

Mit a cut from his razor-edge sabre,
  Hans marked him avay mit de dead:
De draw-cut he often hafe practise
  Vitch trop off de trompeter's head.
Und as on de snow it vent rollin
  Hans dink vot Æsopus have say,
Of trompéters vot plow dirry day neh,
  Mit ton dirry don dir on day.

Like lightnin Hans grab at de trumpet
  Pefore it vas fall to his veet,
Und sharp, mit a derrible blarin,
  He plowed de Französish retreat.
Dis vas shoost ash de Uhlans coom dashin,
  So de Fräntschmen redreaded dat day,
Mit a ron dirry don dy ron day neh,
  Und don dirry don di ron dé.

Dis song is de song of de Teuton
  Vot toot on a trumpet so loud,
Und der Breitmann dat day vas de tutor
  Who teach a new drick to de crowd.
It ish goot for to plow your own trumpet,
  Vas all dat der Breitmann vouldt say,
Mit his don dirry don dy ron day neh,
  Und don dirry don dy ron dé.

GLOSSARY.

Abendgold, (German)—Evening gold.
Abendsonnenschein, (German)—Evening sunshine.
Ach Fuderland, &c., (German)—
"Oh Fatherland how far art thou!
Oh Time—how art thou long!"
Ach weh—An exclamation of pain.
Allatag, (German)—Every day.
Allaweil, (German)—Always; also whilst.
Alles wird ewig zu eins, (German)—And all for ever becomes one.
Alter Schwed', (old Swede)—A familiar phrase, like old fellow.
Anamile, (American)—Animal.
Annerthalb Yar, *Anderthalb Gahr*, (German)—Year and a half.
Anti Word; Antwort—Answer.
Antworded, (German)—Answered.
Arbeiterhalle—Workingman's hall.
Arminius, (Herman.)—The Duke of the Cheruskans, and destroyer of the Roman legions under Varus, in Teutoburg Forest.
Aroom, *Herum*—Around.
Aufgespannt, (German)—Stretched, bent.
Augenblick, (German)—Twinkling of an eye.
Aus, (German)—Out.

Bach, (German)—Brook.
Baender-box—Band-box.
Barrick, (Pennsylvania German for *Berg*,)—Mountain.
Barrel-hell pars—Parallel bars; a part of the gymnastic apparatus.
Be-ghostet, (German, *Begeistert*)—Inspired.
Begifted—Beschenkt.
Begreifen, (German)—Understand.
Beheaded, (German, *Behauptet*)—Asserted.
Bei Leib und Leben, (German)—By my body and soul.
Bekannt Beknown—Known.
Be-mark, (German *Bemerken*)—Observe.
Bemarks, (German, *Bemerkungen*)—Remarks.
Bemerkbar, (German) Observable. (Should be noticed.)
Bemoost, (German)—Mossgrown; in student's language, *ein bemooste Haupt*, an old student.
Bender, (American)—A spree; a frolic. To "go on a *bender*"—to go on a spree.
Be-raised, Raised, with the augment, literal for German *erhoben*.
Berauscht, (German)—Intoxicated.
Besoffen, (German)—Drunk.
Bestimmung des Menschen—Vocation of Man. One of Fichte's works.
Bewises, (German *Beweist*, from *Beweisen*)—Proves.
Bibliothek—Library.
Bix, *Büchse*, (box)—Rifle. Bess in Brown Bess is the equivalent of the German *Büchse*, (Brown being merely an alliterative epithet;) French, *buse tube;* Flemish, *buis*. (Still found in blunderbuss, arquebuss.) See Blackley's "Word Gossip."
Blaetter, (German)—Leaves.
Blei—Lead.
Blitz, (German)—Lightning.
Blitzen, German)—Lightning.
Blokes, (English)—Men.
Bock—A strong kind of German beer.
Boemisch—Bohemian.
Bole Jack road—Near Murfreesboro', Tennessee.

Bool—Bull.

Bornirtheit—Limitedness of capacity.

Bountiee, (American)—Bounty-money paid during the war as a premium to soldiers. To jump the bounty, was to secure the premium and then run away.

"This is the song of Billy Jones,
Who jumped the boun-ti-ee."
American Ballad of 1864.

Bowery—A street in New York, inhabited principally by Germans.

Brav, (German)—Good.

Breit, (German)—Broad.

Bring it down to dots—Reduce it to figures.

Brisner—Prisoner.

Broosh-pinder—Brushbinder, (German, *Buerstenbinder*)—Brushmaker. The brushmakers are supposed, probably on account of their throat-parching business, to be always thirsty.

Brummed, (German, *Crummer*)—To make a growling, deep bass sound.

Bummer, (American)—A low fellow; applied, during the late civil war in the United States, to hangers-on of the army; probably a corruption of the German *bummler*, (loafer.)

Bumming—From Bummer.

Bushwhackers—Guerillas.

Bust his shell, (American)—Broke his head.

Butterbrod, (German)—Buttered bread.

By—*Nearly*; *Beinahe*—Almost, nearly.

Came—Game.

Canyon, (Spanish, *Cañon*)—A narrow passage between high precipitous banks, formed by mountains or table-lands, often with a river running beneath. These occur in the great Western prairies, in New Mexico, and California.

Carmosine, (German)—Crimson. French—Cramoisie.

Carnadine—Incarnadine. Deep pink or blood red.

Change their lodge—Shift from one "society" to another.

Chroc—An Alemannic hero, who ravaged Gaul. Spoken of by Gregory, of Tours, as Chrocus.
Chunk—A short thick piece of wood, or of anything else; a chump. The word is provincial in England and colloquial in the United States.
Cinder, *Suende*—German for sins.
Comedy—Committee.
Conradin—The last of the imperial house of the Hohenstaufen—beheaded at Naples, in 1268.
Coot—(To cut) a dash, (to come out a "swell,") to dress extravagantly.
Coster—The inventor of the art of printing, according to the Dutch.
Crate—Great.
Crislies—Grisly, (bear.)
Da ist er! Schau!—There he is! look!
Damit, (German)—By that.
Das war des Breitmann's Noth, (German)—That was Breitmann's need or fatal extremity. Imitated from the last line of Der Nibelungen Lied.
Deck—The cards used in a game.
Demperanceler, *Temperenzler*—Temperance man.
De Schœnheitsidéal, (German)—The ideal of beauty.
Dessauerinn—A woman from Dessau.
Deutschfertig, (German) — German-ready. A burlesque word. "Then you will be German-ready for an ideal perfect language."
Deutschland—Germany.
Die wile es möhte leben, (Old German, or Middle High German of the 11th century)—During all its life:—

"Daz wolde er immer dienen
Die wile er möhte leben."
Kutrun, xv avent, 756 verse.

Dink—He, they think; *my dinks*—my thoughts.
Dinked—He, they thought.
Dishtriputet—Instead of *attributed.*
Dissembulatin'—Dissembling.
Dissolfed—Instead of *resolved.*
D'lusion—Instead of *allusion.*

Donnered, (German)—Thundered.
Donnerwetter, (German)—Thunder and lightning.
Dooks—Ducks.
Doon—Tune.
Doonderblix—Thunder and lightning.
Drawed he in—(Literal rendering of the German *Zog er ein*) —*Einziehen*, to take up one's abode with.
Dreimal, (German)—Three times.
Drocks—Drakes, dragons; (German)—Drachen.
Druckerei, (German)—Printing office.
Du bist ein Musikant—Thou art a musician.
Dummehrlichkeit, (German)—Honest simplicity.
Eberschwein, (German)—Wild boar.
Einander to *sprechen mit*, (German)—To speak together.
Eldern, (German, *Eltern*)—Parents.
Elders, (German, *Eltern*)—Parents.
Elfenbein, (German)—Ivory.
Emerich—King Emerich, hero of a German legend.
Emsig gruebler, (German)—Assidious inquirer; plodding old fogy.
Entlang, (German)—Along.
Erfounden, (German, *Erfunden*)—Invented.
Ergeben, (German)—Given over. Resigned.
Ernsthaft, (German)—Earnest.
Error-dom, *Irrthum*—Error.
Erstarrt, (German)—Aghast.
Erstaunished, *erstaunt*—Astonished!
Erwaitin', (German, *Erwartend*)—Awaiting, expecting.
Euchred—From Euchre, a Western game of cards.
Fackel Tanz, (German)—Torch dance.
Fancy crabs—Fast horses.
Fanes, *Wetterfahnen*—Weathercocks, (double entente.)
Fass, (German)—Barrel.
Fat—Printer's term.
Feldwebel, (German)—A sergeant.
Fichte—German philosopher.
Finster, (German)—Dark, dismal.
Foll—To fall.
Foal—Full.

Foon—Fun.
Foors—First.
Fore-by—Literal translation of the German *Vorbei.*
Fore-lying—Literal translation of *Vorliegend.*
Foreschlag, (German, *Vorschlag*)—Proposal.
Foresetzen—To set, put (lay) before an audience.
Frau, (German)—Woman.
Freie, (German)—Free.
Freischarlinger, (German, *Freischaerler*)—A member of a free corps; especially applied to those who belonged to the Free Corps formed in Southern Germany during the revolution in 1848.
Freischuetz, (German)—Free shot; one who shoots with charmed bullets; the name of Karl Maria Von Weber's celebrated opera.
Friederich Rothbart—Frederic Barbarossa, the great emperor of Germany, and one of the German Legendary heroes. He is supposed to sleep in the Kyffnauser in Thuringia, and to awaken one day, when he will bring great glory over Germany.
Frolic—Fröhlich, merry.
Froze to de ready—Held fast to the money.
Fullenden, (German, *Vollenden*)—To finish, perfect.
Fuss, (German)—Foot.
Fust—The partner of Gutemberg, the inventor of the art of printing.
Gambrinus—A mythical king of Brabant, supposed to have been the inventor of beer.
Gandertate—Candidate.
Ganz, (German)—Entirely.
Ganz und gar, (German)—Altogether; all over.
Gast, (German)—Guest.
Gauer—Vallies.
Gaul dern—A Yankee oath.
Gauner-sprache, (German)—Thieves' language.
Ge-birt', (German, *Geburt*)—Birth.
Ge-bildet—Built, with the German augment.
Geborn—Born, with the augment.
Ge-brudert, (formed like ge-schwister.)—Brothers.

Geh hin mein Puch, (German of 16th century.)
Gehst nit mit rechten Dingen zu—Dost not do it by any natural means; there is witchcraft in it.
Gekommene—Arrived, (newly arrived.)
Gekommen so, (German)—Come thus.
Gelbschnabel, (German)—Yellow bill, (*i. e.* soft.) Meaning a "greenhorn."
Gelt, (German, *Geld*)—Money.
Gemüthlichkeit, (German)—Good nature; a cheerful tone of mind.
Gensy broost, (German, *Gänsebrust*)—Goose-breast.
Ge-roasted—Roasted, with German augment.
Gesembled—Assembled, with the augment of the German preterite.
Geshmasht—Smashed, with German augment.
Gespicked, (German)—Larded.
Gestohlen und bekannt, (German)—Stolen, and known.
Gesundheit, (German)—Health.
Gesangverein, (German)—Singing-society.
Geskostet—Cost, with the German augment.
Gilt—In the ordinary sense, and also in the same verse, "*gilt*," implying the meaning of the German verb "*gelten*," to be worth something and *guilt*.
Glaub'es, (German)—Believe it.
Glee-wine, *Gluhwein*—Hot spiced wine.
Glueck, (German)—Luck.
Glucky, (German, *Gluecklich*)—Lucky.
Goblum—For goblin.
Gool—Cool.
Go screech, *Geschrei*—Bawling, clamour.
Gott-full, *gottvoll*—Glorious, divine.
Gottallmachty, (German, *Gottallmächtig*)—God Almighty.
Gotteshaus, (German)—House of God.
Gott weiss, (German)—Heaven knows!
Gottsdonnerkreuzschockschwerenoth, (German)—Another variety of big swearing.
Gott's-doonder, (German, *Gott's Donner*)—God's thunder. See also *Gott's tausend*, a thundering sort of oath, but never preceded by lightning, for it is only used as a

kind of expletive to express great surprise, or to give great emphasis to words which, without it, would seem to be capable of none.

Gottstausend, (German)—An abbreviation of *Gott's tausend Donnerwetter*, (God's thousand thunders,) and therefore the comparative of *Gott's doonder;* with most of those who use it, a meaningless phrase.

Go von—Go one ; bet on him.

Grillers—Guerillas.

Grod, *gerard*—Straight.

Gross, (German)—Great.

Guestfriendllick, *gastfreundlich*—Hospitable.

Gummi lasticum—India Rubber.

Gutemberg—The inventor of the art of printing.

Guve—Southern slang for give. *Guv*, for give, is also English slang as well as American.

Gyrotwistive—Snaky.

Hand-shoe, (German, *Handschuh*)—Glove.

Hanserl, (German)—Jacky.

Hans Wurst—Merry Andrew ; Zani ; Jack Pudding—the latter word being a literal translation of the German Hans Wurst ; the pudding in either case referring to the sausages, or the pretended sausages, which the Merry Andrew always appeared to be swallowing by the yard or fathom. See *Blackley's Word Gossip.*

Hagel! Blitz! Kreuz Sakrament! (German)—Another variety of swearing.

Haul te pot—Take the stakes.

Hause—House.

Heavy—Hood.

Hegel—Name of the German philosopher.

Heine, *Heinrich*—German poet.

Heini von Steier—Heinrich von Opterdingen.

Heldenbuch—Is the title of a collection of epic poems, belonging to the cycle of the German Saga.

Heller Glorie schein—Bright gloriole.

Heller, (German)—*Farthing.*

Hereauf, *hierauf*—Thereupon.

Herout, (German, *Heraus*)—Out.

Herrlich, (German)—Noble; lordly.

Herr Je, (German)—An abbreviation of *Herr Jesus* (O Lord!); generally used only by those who are fond of meaningless exclamations.

Hexerei—Witchery, sorcery.

Hertszen—Herzen; hearts.

Hertzhog, *Herzog*, (German)—Duke.

Herzlich, (German)—Heartily; cordially.

Himmel, (German)—Heaven.

Himmels-Potz-Pumpen-Herrgott—A mild sort of a German imprecation, untranslatable.

Himmlisch-hoellisch qual, (German)—Heavenly-hellish pain.

Hobbiness—Happiness.

Hoellisch, (German)—Hellish.

Honey foolin', *Honeyfuggle*—Is believed to be English slang. In America it means blarneying, deceiving.

Hoockle perry, Persimmoned—"A huckleberry over my persimmon." Surpassed; outdone.

Hoof-irons, (*Huf-eisen* in German)—Horse-shoe.

Hop-sossa, (German) int.—Hop; heyday.

Hundsfott, (German *Vulg.*)—Mean scoundrel; hound.

Hunk, (American)—Stout, solid, profitable.

I Gili romaneskro. This song is written in the German-Gipsy dialect. *Eh'* in the third line of the second verse is the German word ehe, (ere or before.) *Kuribente*, (in war,) is in the Slavonic and Gipsy *local* case, or as Pott calls it—(*Die Zigennen in Europa und Asia*)—The second dative. Pasputi, following Puchmayer, calls it the first dative, as *e rakleste* "in the child."

Im gruenen Wald, (German)—In the green wood.

Im Oaken Wald, (German)—In the oak wood.

In nomine Domine, (Latin)—In the name of the Lord;

"In nomine Domine!
Was Hero Hagen's word."

In Sang und Klang dein Lebenlang. In song and music all thy life.

Jeff, (printer's phrase)—A game played by throwing up types and counting the nicks.

Joss-stick—A name given to small reeds, covered with the dust of odoriferous woods, which the Chinese burn before their idols.
Jours—Journeymen.
Jungfernkranz, (German)—Bridal garland.
Kœnig Etzel—King Attila.
Kaiser Karl—Charlemagne.
Kalt, (German)—Cold.
Kanaster, (German)—Canaster tobacco.
Karfunkelstein, (German)—Carbuncle.
Kartoffell, (German)—Potato.
Kauder-Waelsch, (German)—Gibberish.
Kellner, (German)—Waiter.
Kinder, (German)—Children.
Kitin, *a kitin*—Flying or running rapidly.
Knasterbart, (German)—Literally, tobacco-beard; a tough, old bearded, old-fashioned fellow.
Kneiperei, (German)—Revel.
Knock dem out de shpots—Knock the spots out of them; astonish.
Komm maideiein! Rothe Waengelein, (German)—Come, maiden, red cheeks.
Kop, (German *Kopf*)—Head.
Kreutzer,—Fr. Creutzer, distinguished professor in the University of Heidelberg, author of a great work on "Symbolik."
Kreuzfidél, (German)—True-hearted; gallant in the highest degree.
Krumm, (German)—Crooked. *Breit und Krumm*—Broad and crooked. Here, a pun on bride and groom.
Kümmel, (German) Cumin brandy.
Kummel Kimmel, (German)—Schnapps; dram.
Lager, *Lagerbeer*, (German *Lagerbier*, i. e. *Stockbeer*.)
Lager Wirthschaft, (German)—Beerhouse.
Lam—To drub; to beat soundly.
Lateinisch—Latin.
Laughen, *lachen*—Laughing.
Lavergne—A place between Nashville and Murfreesboro', in the State of Tennessee.

Lebenlang, (German)—Lifelong.
Leider, *Leids*, (German)—Songs.
Libby—The notorious Confederate prison at Richmond, Va.
Liddle Pills—Legislative enactments.
Liederkranz, (German)—Glee-union.
Liederlich, (German)—Loose, reckless, dissolute.
Lighthood, (German *Lichtheif*)—Licht.
Like spiders down their webs—Breitmann's soldiers are supposed to have been expert turners or gymnasts.
Loafer—A term which, considered as the German pronunciation of *lover*, is a close translation of *rom*, as this latter means both a Gipsy and a husband.
Loosty, (German *Lustig*)—Jolly: merry.
Los, *los gehen*, (German)—To go at a thing, at somebody.
Loudet, (*Lauten* in German)—To make sound.
Lump, (German)—Ragamuffin.
Lumpenglocke, (German)—An abusive term applied to bells, especially to those which give the signal that the beer houses must close.
Maedchen, (German)—Girl; maiden.
Mákana, (Gipsy, *Ma akana*)—But now.
"*Make de red cock crow*"—"To set the red cock on the roof," signifies in German, to set a man's house on fire.
Marmorbild—Marble statue.
Markgraefler—A pleasant light wine grown in the Duchy of Baden.
Maskenzug, (German)—Procession of masked persons.
Massenversammlung, (German)—Mass meeting.
Mein Freund—My Friend.
Meine Seel', (German)—By my soul.
Mineted—Minded.
Minnesinger—Poet of love; a name given to German lyric poets, who flourished from the twelfth to the fourteenth centuries.
Mit hoontin knife, &c.—

"With her white hands so lovely
She dug the Count his grave,
From her dark eyes sad weeping,
The holy water she gave."

(Old German ballad.)

Mitout—Without
Mitternocht, *Mitternacht*—Midnight.
Mitternight, *Mitternacht*—Midnight.
Mitz hauf, (German)—Dung-hill.
Moleschott—Author of a celebrated work on Physiology.
Morgan—John Morgan, a notorious Confederate guerilla during the late war in America.
Morgen-het-ache—Morning headache.
Moskopolite—(American)—Cosmopolite.
Murmulte—Murmured.
Mutter, (German)—Mother.
Nieblungen Lied—The lay of the Nieblungen; the great German national epos.
Nix, (German, *Nichts*)—Nothing.
Nix cum raus—Had not come out.
Norate—To speak in an oration.
No sardine—Not a narrow-minded, small-hearted fellow.
Noth, (German)—Need, dire extremity. Das war des Breitmann's noth. That was Breitmann's sore trial. Imitated from the last line of the *Niebelungen Lied.*
Nun—Now.
Nun-endich, (German)—Well, at last.
O'Brady—An Irish giant commemorated in a once popular song.
Oder—Other.
Odenwald—A thickly-wooded district in South Germany.
Ohne Zhal, (German)—Without number.
On-belongs—Literal translation of *Zugehört.*
On-did, to *on-do*—Literal translation of the German anthem; *to dun*, to put on.
On de snap—All at once.
Onfang, (German, *Anfang*)—Beginning.
Oonshpeakbarly, (German, *unanssprechbarlich*)—Inexpressibly.
Oonendly—Undenlich.
Oop-geclearéd, (German, *Aufgeklaert*)—Enlightened.
Oopright-hood, (German, *Aufrichtigkeit*)—Uprightness.
Ooprighty, (German, *Aufrichtig*)—Upright.
Oopshtardet, (German, *Aufgeschärft*)—Upstarted.

Oop-sproong—For *aufsprung.*
Orgel-ton, (German)—Organ sound.
Orkester—Orchestra.
Out-sprach—Outspoke.
Out-signed, (German, *ausgezeichnete*)—Distinguished, signal.
Over again—*Uebringen*—The remainder; a rest.
Pabst, Der Pabst lebt, &c.—" The Pope he leads a happy life," &c., beginning of a popular German song.
Peeps—People. "Hard on the American peeps"—a phrase for anything exacting or severely pressing.
Pelznickel, Nick, Nickel!—St. Nicolas is supposed, on the night preceding his name-day, the sixth of December, to pass over the house-tops on his long-eared steed, having baskets suspended on either side filled with sweets and playthings, and to drop down through the chimneys presents for those children who have been good during the year, but birch-rods for those who have been naughty, would not go to bed early, or objected to being washed, &c. In the expectation of his coming, the children put, on the eve of St. Nicolas day, either a shoe, or a stocking, or a little basket into the chimney-piece of their parents' bed-room. We may remark, by the way, that St. Nicolas is the Christian successor of the heathen Nikudr, of ancient German mythology. In America he has become confused with Christkinder and Christkinkel.
Pesser, besser, (German)—Better.
Pestain—Stain, with the augment.
Pfaelzer—A man from the Rhenish Palatinate.
Pfeil, (German)—Arrow.
Philosopede—Velocipede.
Pie the forms—Break up and scatter the forms of type.
Pig-sticker, (American)—Bowie-knife, or indeed, any other kind of knife.
Pile out, (American)—Hurry out.
Plue goats—Blue coats; soldiers.
Plug muss, (American Fireman)—A fight around a fire-plug.

Pokal, (Poculum)—Goblet.
Poker—A favorite game of cards among Western gamblers.
Poonkin—Pumpkin.
Potzausend! Was ist das?—Zounds! What is that?
Potzblitz, (German)— int., The deuce.
Poulterie—Poultry.
Poussiren—To court.
Pretzel, (German)—A kind of fancy bread, twist or the like.
Prezackly—Pre(cisely,) exactly.
Protocollirt, *protocolliren*—To register, record.
Pumpernickel—A heavy, hard sort of rye-bread.
Pye—To buy.
Raushlin', *rauschend*—Rustling.
Reb—An abbreviation of rebel.
Redakteur—Editor.
Rede, (German)—Speech.
Rede, (German)—Speech.
Red-Waelsch, *Roth-Wae sch*, (German)—Thieves' language.
Reiter, (German)—Rider.
Rheinweinbechers Klang—The Rhine wine goblet's sound.
Richter, (Jean Paul, French)—Distinguished German author.
Ridersmann, (*Reitersmann* in German)—Rider.
Ring—A political clique or cabal.
Ritter, (German)—Knight.
Roland—One of the paladins of Charlemagne.
Rollin' locks—Rolling logs; mutually aiding.
Rosen, (German)—Roses.
Rouse, (German *Heraus*)—Out; come out.
Sachsen—Saxonia, Saxony.
Sacrin—Consecrating.
Sagen Cyclus—Cycle of legends.
Sass, *Sassy*, *Sassin'*—Sauce, saucy, &c.
Sauerkraut, (German)—Sour krout.
Sauerkraut, (German)—Pickled cabbage.
Saw it—Understood it.
Scatterin, *Scotterin*—Scattering.
Schauer, (German)—Shudder.
Schenk aus, (German) Pour out.

Schenket ein, (German)—Pour in, (fill the glasses.)
Schimmel, (German)—Grey horse.
Schimpft und flucht gar laesterlich, (German)—Swears and blasphemes abominally.
Schinken, (German)—Ham.
Schläger, (German)—A kind of sword or broadsword; a rapier used by students for duelling or fighting matches.
Schlesierwein, (German)—Wine grown in Silesia, proverbially sour.
Schlimmer, (German)—Worse.
Schlished, *geschlitzt*—Slit.
Schlop him ober de kop—Knocked him on the head.
Schlopped—Slopped.
Schloss, (German)—Castle.
Schnapps, (German)—Dram.
Schnitz—Pennsylvania German word for cut and dried fruit.
Schnitz, *schnitzen*, (German)—To chop, chip, snip. In Pennsylvania *Schnitz* or *Snits*, is applied to cut and dried fruit, apples, pears, or peaches. It was, I believe, Prof. Henry Coppée, who narrated, in Lippincott's Magazine, a story to the effect that a school teacher once asked his class if an apple were cut in two, what would the pieces be called? "Halves," replied the boys. "And if cut again?" "Quarters." "And then cut again?" "*Snitz*," was the unanimous answer.
Schönheitsidéal, (German)—The ideal of beauty.
Schopenhauer—A celebrated German "philosophical physiologist."
Schoppen, (German)—A liquid measure, chopin, pint.
Schwaben—Suabia.
Schwanen, (German)—Swans.
Schwartzer Mohr, (German)—A black negro. Mohr in German is applied very generally to both Moors and negroes.
Schweinblatt—(Swine) Dirty paper.
Schweitzer kase, (German)—Swiss cheese.
Schwig, *Swig*, verb—To drink by large draughts.
Schwigs, *Swig* noun—A large draught.

Scmysed, (German *Schmyssen*, from *Schmeissen*)—Threw him out of doors.
Scoop—Take in; get.
Scorched—Escorted; a negro malapropism.
Scrouged, (American)—Pressed, jammed.
Seelen—Ideal. Soul's ideal.
Sefen-lefen—Seven or eleven.
Seifenblasen—Soap balls.
Seins, (German)—The Being.
Selbstanchauungsvermögen, (German)—Capacity for self-inspection.
Serenity—A transparency.
Shanty—A board cabin; slang for house.
Shapel—Chapel is an old word for a printing-office.
Sharman, *Sherman*—German.
Shings—Jingo; by Jingo.
Shipsy—Gipsy.
Shlide—Slide. "Let it slide," vulgar for "let it go."
Shnow-wice, (German *Schnee-weis*)—Snow-white.
Shoopider—Jupiter.
Shootin-stick—Shooting stick. It is used for closing up the forms of types.
Show-spiel, *Schauspiel*—Play; piece.
Shpeck—*Speck*, (German)—Bacon.
Shpicket—Spigot; a pin or peg to stop a small hole in a cask of liquor.
Shpoons—Spoons; plunder.
Shtuhl, (German *Stuhl*)—Stool; chair.
Sinn, (German)—Meaning.
Six mals—Six times.
Skeeted—Went fast; skated (?)
Skool—Skull.
Skyugle, (American)—"Skyugle" is a word which had a short run during 1864. It means many things, but chiefly to disappear or to make disappear. Thus a deserter "skyugled," and sometimes he "skyugled a coat or watch."
Slanganderin'—Foolishly slandering.
Slasher gaffs—Spurs for cocks with cutting edges.

Slibowitz—A Bohemian Schnapps distilled from plums.
Slop over—Go too far and upset or spill. Applied to men who venture too far in a success.
Slumgoozlin'—Slum or slum-guzzling ; humbug.
Slumgullion—A Mississippi term for a legislator.
Solidaten, (German *Soldaten*)—Soldiers.
So mit, (German)—Thus with.
Sonntags, (German)—Sundays.
Sottelet, (German *Gesattelt*)—Saddled.
Sound upon the goose—A phrase originating in the Kansas troubles, and signifying true to the cause of slavery.
Souse and Brouse, (German *Saus und Braus*)—Revelry and rioting.
Spiel, (German)—Play.
Splodderin'—Splattering.
Spook, (German *Spuk*)—A ghost.
Sporn, (German)—Spur.
Sports—Sporting men.
Staub, (German)—Dust.
Stein, (German)—Stone.
Stille, (German)—Stillness.
Stim, (German *Stimme*)—Voice.
Stohr—Store.
Straight flush—In poker, all the cards of one suit.
Strassen, (German)—Streets.
Strauss—Name of the celebrated Viennese composer.
Strumpf, (German)—Stocking.
Studenten in den Gassen, (German)—Students in the streets or lanes.
Sturm und Drang, (German)—Storm and pressure.
Sweynheim und Pannarts—The first printers at Rome.
Takes, (printer's phrase)—Allotments of copy, or strips, to each printer.
Tantzen, (German)—To dance.
Tantz, (German)—Dance.
Tarnal—Eternal.
Taub, *taube*, (German)—Dove.
Taugenix, *Taugenichts*—Good-for-nothing fellow.
Theil, (German)—Part.

Thoom—Thumb.
Thrip, (South American)—Three pence.
Thusnelda—The wife of Arminius, (Hermann.)
Tod, (German)—Dead.
Todtengrips, *Todtengerippe*—Skeleton.
Tofe—Dove.
To House, (German *zu Hause*)—At home.
Tortled—To tortle; to move off. From *turtle*.
Touch the dirt—Touch the road.
Treppe, (German)—Stairs.
Treu, (German)—Faithful, true.
Trow him with ecks—Pelt him with eggs.
Turner, (German)—Gymnast.
Turner Verein, (German *Turnverein*)—Gymnastic Society.
Tyfel, *Teufel*—Devil.
Tyfeled, *Verteufelt*—Devilish.
Tyfel-schnake, *Teufelschnaken* — Deviltries; also devil-snake.
Tyful-strikes, *Teufel-streiche*—Devilstrokes.
Tyful-wards—Devilwards.
Tyfelest—From Teufel: here in the sense of "best" or "worst."
Ueberschwengliche, (German)—Transcendental; elevated.
Ueber Stein and Schwein, (German)—Over stone and swine.
Ulievrus—Oliver, another of the twelve Paladins of Charlemagne who fell at Roncesvalles, (A Rowland for an Oliver.)
Und lauter guter Ding, (German)—And of thoroughly good cheer.
Urbummellied, (German *vulgar*)—Arch-loafer's song; a student song.
Urlied, (German)—The song of yore.
Van't klein komt men tot't groote, (Dutch)—Great things may have small beginnings. (Concordia res parvae cresrunt)—Legend on the Dutch ducats.
Varus—The Roman Commander in Germany, conquered by Arminius.
Verdammt, (German)—D——d.

Verfluchter, (German)—Accursed.
Verstay, *Verstehen*—Understand.
Vertyfeln, *Verteufeln*—To botch.
Verloren, (German)—Forlorn.
Versteh, *verstehen* (German)—To understand.
Voonderly, (German) *Wunderlich*—Wondrous; curious.
Von—One.
Wachsen, (German)—Grow:—

> "Komm'ich in's galante Sachsen,
> Wo di schœne Maedchen wachsen."
>
> Old German Song.

Waechter, (German)—Watchman.
Waelder, (German)—Woods.
Wahlverwandtschaft, (German)—Elective affinity; sympathy of souls.
Wahrsagt, (German *Wahrsagen*)—To foretell, soothsay.
Wahres Kunstgenuss, (German)—Truly artistic enjoyment.
Waidmanncheil, (German)—Huntsman's weal, or greeting.
Ward al zu Steine, (German)—Became all stone.
Ward zu Wind, (German)—Became a wind.
Wechsebalg, (German)—A changeling; brat; urchin.
Weihnachtstbaum, (German)—Christmas tree.
Weiknachtslied, (German)—Christmas song.
Weingeist, (German)—Vinous; ardent spirit.
Wein-handle, (German *Weinhandlung*)—Wineshop.
Weinnachtstraum—lit., Winenight's dream; for "Weienacht," Christmas dream.
Wellen and Wogen, (German)—Waves and billows.
Welshhen—Turkey hen.
Werden das Werden—The becoming to be.
We'uns, you'uns—We and you. A common vulgarism through the Southern States.

> "'Tis sad that we,uns from you'uns parts,
> When you'uns have stolen we'uns hearts."

Wie gehts, (German)—How goes it? how are you?
Wild Jagd—Wild hunt.
Wild un weh, (German)—Wild and woe-begone.
Wilkomm, (German)—Welcome.

Windsbraut, (German poet)—Storm; hurricane; gust of wind.
Wird, (German)—Becomes.
Wised, (German *Wusste*, from *Wizzen*)—Knew.
Witz, (German)—A sally, or witty saying.
Wo bist du? (German)—Where art?
Woe-moaedy, (German *Wemüthing)*—Moanful, doleful
Wohl, (German)—Well!
Wohl auf! (German)—Literally well up; but meaning "*hey!*" or "up there!"
Wolfsschlucht, (German)—Wolf's glen.
Wonnevol, (German *Wonnevoll*)—Blissful.
Woon, (German *Wunde*)—Wound.
Word-blay—Word-play; pun; quibble.
Wurst, (German)—Sausage.
Wurst mir und égal,—All one to me. Wurst is a German student word for indifference.
Yaeger, (German)—Huntsmen.
Yaegersmann, *Faegersmann*—Huntsman.
Yartausend, *Jahrtausend*—A thousand years.
Yartausend, *Jahrtausend*, (German)—A thousand years.
Yellow pine, (American)—A mulatto.
Youngest Day, (German)—Juengste tag. The Day of Judgment.
Yungling, *Jüngling*, (German)—Youth.
Zimmer, (German)—Room.
Zupfet aus, (German)—Tap the barrel.

GLOSSARY.

Abenddämmerung, (German)—Evening dim light; twilight.
Abendroth, (German)—Evening red.
Abbordez-moi vodre métre, (German-French)—Bring me your mayor.
Allegader—All together.
Appletods, (American)—Apple toddies.
Armlos—Unarmed.
Arrèire pensée, (French)—A reserved thought or intention.
Augen, (German)—Eyes.
Baldface corn, (American)—Plain maize whisky.
Bauern, German)—Peasants.
Bellin, (German *Bellen*,)—To bark.
Bemarket, (German English)—Remarked.
Betaubend, (German)—Enchanting.
Bienenkorb, (German)—Beehive.
Birra gazzosa, (Italian)—Ærated, gaseous beer.
Bischof, (German)—Bishop.
Boerenvolk, (Flemish)—Peasants.
Bouleverse—Boulevard.
Branntewein, (German)—Spirits.
Brandy smash, (American)—A plain half-glass mint julep of only sugar, ice, spirits, and mint. A regular julep is larger, and contains more ingredients.
Brücke, (German)—Bridge.
Bugs—In America all insects, especially Coleoptera.
Camine—Chimney-piece.

Carmagnole—A wild street dance.
Clam—The popular name of a bivalvular shell-fish, the *Venus.*
Clavier, (German)—Piano.
Colle belle, (Italian)—With the beauties.
Corned, (American)—Made drunk.
Crecian pend—When Breitmann says "Dat pend of the bow ish the Crecian pend," it is a rather equivocal compliment. "Grecian bend" has lately become a common newspaper expression. Smuggling done by women is called a "Case of Grecian bend." The present style of skirt, full at the back, is favorable to it.
Dampfschiff—Steamboat.
Dunkelheit—Darkness.
Dursty, (German *Durstig*)—Thirsty.
Earnsthaft, ernsthaft—Serious.
Eber, (German)—Wild boar.
Eckhartshausen—A German supernaturalist.
Eher, (German)—Sooner. In the dialect it has the meaning of "before."
Engel, (German)—Angel.
Engländrinn, (German)—English woman.
Erfinder, (German)—Inventor.
Euchre, Eucre—Sort of game played with cards, very much in vogue in the West.
Feinslieb, (German)—Fair or fine love.
Foxen, (German *Fuchsen*)—Foxes.
Frank-tiroir—Franc-tireur.
François Villon—An old French humorous poet, whom Boileau speaks of as the first who began to write truly modern French.
Garce, (French)—Wench.
Gar nichts, (German)—Not at all.
Gass und Strass, (German)—Lane and street.
Gasbalgs—Bladder of gas.
Gaul darn—G———n.
Gestohlen—Stolen.
Gewehr, (German)—Musket.
Gift, (German)—Poison.

Glamour—Ocular deception ; by magic.
Gottashe—Cottage.
Gott weiss, (German)—God knows.
Hab' und Güter, (German)—Property.
Halberthier, for *Halberdier*—Halberthier means half an animal.
Hans Michel—A popular, but not complimentary name for Germany.
Harmlos, (German)—Harmless.
Herzbruder, (German)—Heart's brother.
Hoofstad, (Flemish)—Capital.
Hut, (German)—Hat.
Ik leven, (Flemish)—I live.
Ildiavolo in carnato, (Italian)—The devil incarnate, or in carnation.
In geburst—Burst.
Ita dixit, (Latin)—So said.
Kan ik. Ik kan, (Flemish)—I can.
Kermes—Annual Fair.
Kitin, a kitin—Flying or running rapidly.
Kloster, (German)—Cloister.
Kœnig Etzel—King Attila.
Kong (German *König*)—Old Norse for king.
Kooken—Cake.
Kopf, (German)—Head.
Küster, (German)—Sacristan.
Lanze, (German)—Lance.
Lai bgartner, (German)—Leibgard ; bodyguard. The Swiss in blundering makes it "body gardener."
Larmen—The French word *larmes*, tears, made into a German verb.
Leben—Life ; living.
Lebendig, (German)—Living.
Lev'st du nock?—Livs't thou yet?
Lieblich, (German)—Charming.
Liedeken, (Flemish)—Song.
Losbinden—Tie a dog loose.
L' Ubbriacone, (Italian)—Drunkard.
Luftballon, (German)—Air-balloon.

Madel, (German)—Girl.
Meisjes, (Flemish)—Girls.
Mijn lief gesellen, (Flemish)—My dear comrades.
Mohr, ein schwarzer, (German) —A blackamoor.
Mondenlight—Moonlight.
Mondenschein, (German)—Moonlight.
Mud-sill—The longitudinal timber laid upon the ground to form the foundation for a railway. Hence figuratively applied by the labor-despising Southern gentry to the laboring classes as the substratum of society.
Naturalizationisds—The officers, &c., who give the rights of native citizens to foreigners.
Nieuw Jarsie—New Jersey, in America, famous *inter alia* for its sandy beaches and high surf.
Nig—Nigger.
Nirwana—The Brahminical absorption into God.
Ochsen, (German)—Oxen ; stupid fellows. As a verb it also is used familiarly to mean hard study.
Oltra tramontane ; ultra tramontane—Applied to the non-Italian Catholic party.
Out-ge-poke-te—Out-poked.
Paardeken, (Flemish)—Palfrey.
Palact, (German *Pallast*)—Palace.
Péké—Belgian rye whisky.
Pickel-haube, (German)—The spiked helmet worn by Prussian soldiers.
Pimeby—By and by.
"*Plain*"—Water plain, *i. e.*, unmixed.
Pully, i. e., Bully,—An Americanism, adjective. Fine, capital. A slang word, used in the same manner as the English used the word *crack ;* as, "a *bully* horse," "a *bully* picture."
Put der Konig troo—To put through, (American,) to qualify, to imitate.
Red cock—Or make de red cock crow. Einem den rothen Hahn auf's Dach setzen. A German proverb signifying to set fire to a house.
Reiten gaen, (Flemish)—Go riding.
Reiver—Robber.

Reue, (German)—Repentance.
Rheingraf, (German)—Count of the Rhine districts.
Ringe, (German)—Rings.
Rolette—Roulette.
Schatz—Sweetheart.
Schauer, (German)—Awe.
Schmutz, (German)—Dirt.
Schwer, (German)—Heavy.
Schweinpig, (German)—Swinepig.
Selfe, (German *Selbe*)—Same.
Shpicket—Spigot; a pin or peg to stop a small hole in a cask of liquor.
Shlide, (American)—Depart.
Shlished, *geschlitzt*—Slit.
Shlopped—Slopped.
Shmysed, (German *Schmissen*, from *Schmeissen*)—Threw him out of doors.
Silbern, (German)—Silver.
Speck, (German)—Bacon.
Spielman, (German)—Musician.
Squander, (American)—Wander. Used in this sense in "The Big Bear of Arkansas."
Stone fence, (American)—Rye whisky.

> "I went in and got a horn
> Of old stone fence."
> —*Jim Crow*, 1832.

Straaten, (Flemish)—Streets.
Stunden, (German)—Leagues. About 4½ English miles.
Teufelsjagersmann—Devil's huntsman.
Tiger—An American term for a gambling table.
Tixey—"I wish I was in Dixie." The origin of this song is rather curious. Although now thoroughly adopted as a Southern song, and "Dixey's Land" understood to mean the Southern States of America, it was, some 75 years ago, the estate of one Dixie, on Manhattan Island, who treated his slaves well; and it was their lament, on being deported south, that is now known as "I wish I was in Dixie."

Turchin—Colonel Turchin's men ravaged the town of Huntsville (Ala.) during the civil war.
Ueberschwengliche, (German)—Transcendental; elevated.
Uhr, (German)—Clock, watch, hour, time. Used for "hour" in the ballad.
Uhu, (German)—Owl.
Un-windoong, (German Entwicklung?)—Unravelling.
Unvollkommene technik—Unfinished style or method.
Veilchen, (German)—Violets.
Vercieren, (Flemish)—Adorn; exalt.
Villiam—Willam Street at New York, inhabited by many Germans.
Vlaemsche—Flemish.
Vorüber, (German)—Past.
Wachsen, (German)—Waxen.
Wald, (German)—Wood.
Wallowin—Walloon.
Wälschen, (German)—Of the Latin race.
Weingarts, weingärten, (German)—Vineyards.
Werda? (German)—Who's there.
Wise-hood, (German *Weisheit*)—Wisdom.
Yager, (Jager, German)—Hunter.
Yar, (German *Jahr*)—Year.
Yonge maegden, (Flemish)—Young girls.
Zukunftig, (German)—In future.

www.ingramcontent.com/pod-product-compliance
Lightning Source LLC
LaVergne TN
LVHW020228110826
845151LV00003B/860

* 9 7 8 1 4 2 5 5 3 0 5 7 0 *